in **DETAIL** High-Density Housing

in **DETAIL**

High-Density Housing
Concepts · Planning · Construction

Christian Schittich (Ed.)

Edition Detail – Institut für internationale
Architektur-Dokumentation GmbH & Co. KG
München

Birkhäuser
Basel · Boston · Berlin

Editor: Christian Schittich
Project Manager: Andrea Wiegelmann
Editorial Services: Kathrin Draeger, Alexander Felix, Julia Liese, Christa Schicker

Translation German/English: Elizabeth Schwaiger (pp. 8–43, 168–173),
Catherine Anderle-Neill (pp. 44–167)
Drawings: Kathrin Draeger, Norbert Graeser, Christiane Haslberger,
Oliver Klein, Emese Köszegi, Beate Stingl
DTP: Peter Gensmantel, Cornelia Kohn, Andrea Linke, Roswitha Siegler

A specialist publication from Redaktion DETAIL
This book is a cooperation between
DETAIL – Review of Architecture and
Birkhäuser – Publishers for Architecture

A CIP catalogue record for this book is available
from the Library of Congress, Washington D.C., USA

Bibliographic information published by Die Deutsche Bibliothek
The Deutsche Bibliothek lists this publication in the Deutsche Nationalbibliografie;
detailed bibliographic data is available on the Internet at <http://dnb.ddb.de>.

© 2004 Institut für internationale Architektur-Dokumentation GmbH & Co. KG,
P. O. Box 33 06 60, D-80066 Munich, Germany and
Birkhäuser Verlag AG, Basel · Boston · Berlin, P. O. Box 133, CH-4010 Basel,
Switzerland

Printed on acid-free paper produced from chlorine-free pulp (TCF ∞).

Printed in Germany
Reproduction: Karl Dörfel Reproduktions-GmbH, München
Printing and binding: Kösel GmbH & Co. KG, Altusried-Krugzell

ISBN 978-3-7643-7113-5

9 8 7 6 5 4 3 2

Contents

The Challenge of High-Density Housing

Christian Schittich

Why do we need new concepts for high-density housing, when each inhabitant, in a country like Germany, already has more than 40 m² of living space, when, simultaneously, the population is decreasing, when the countryside is already spoilt by an excess of development and when public opinion polls reveal that everyone dreams of their own little house in the country?

Appearances to the contrary aside: the housing question is far from being solved. The demand is as great as ever. Demand for apartments for specific household configurations and social groups, for apartments that respond to changes in society, and, last but not least, demand for apartments in countless conurbations. For, geographically speaking, the supply of reasonable living space is by no means evenly distributed. Thus in Germany today, entire housing schemes in the East, in the Saar or the Ruhr regions stand vacant, while appropriate housing is an unaffordable luxury in large cities such as Munich, Stuttgart, Hamburg and Cologne. In these cities, commercial investors, led by the powerful real estate funds, still prefer to put their money into glittering office towers or new shopping malls. Despite the risk that they tend to stand vacant at first, due to a glut in the market, they still promise higher returns in the long term. More public incentives are needed to jumpstart new housing construction. Housing that is reasonable and ecological, capable of meeting specific social criteria and responding to changing social conditions.

There is a real phenomenon at play: although social structures have changed considerably in the past decades – with the result that the significance of the average nuclear family continues to decline – the typical apartment floor plan is still almost exclusively designed for the needs of just such a family, even in new developments. It isn't as if today's variety of lifestyles imposes an imperative for specialized floor plans. Rather, what we need are flexible types that make it possible to react to changing life circumstances by simple means.

However, since people seem to be at their most conservative when it comes to housing and since clients tend to choose the path of least resistance, and lower risk, innovations are extremely slow to gain acceptance in the housing sector. While futuristic design and the latest technologies are embraced wholeheartedly in other areas, for automobiles and computers, for example, and also for building tasks such as railway stations, museums or fashion boutiques, housing

ideas and tastes lean towards proven and traditional values. Obviously, this phenomenon has enormous influence on the design, as well as on urban planning and the access and floor plan concept. Developers and investors operate on the basis of fitting the supply to existing demands. The result is often no more than a mass product reduced to average client wishes.

Conversely, progressive architects are often reproached for ignoring the ideas of users and for executing plans that are out of sync with the market. After all, inhabitants do not always respond to innovative floor plan solutions, structural or facade designs with enthusiasm. Appropriate public guidance is vital, especially in terms of implementing necessary innovations. It is more important than ever, therefore, to abandon the principle of "equal shares for all" in the allocation of state subsidies and tax benefits. Not only in order to finally build and promote high-density housing in regions where it is truly needed, in areas where people live and work. But also to create unique incentives for meeting essential criteria that are relevant for the future: sustainable building in the existing fabric, ecological measures, accessibility, the creation of living space for certain marginal groups, and, finally, progressive housing concepts appropriate to our age.

Even today many outstanding projects in apartment housing are being created – thanks to the possibility of gaining partial autonomy from market mechanisms – as demonstration projects that are initiated and supported by the state. Some of the examples in this book illustrate this point. Others originate in initiatives of inhabitants, who form interest or neighbourhood associations or housing co-operatives.
In one case (Wolfram Popp, cf. pp.154) the architect even assumed the role of client. The fact that he quickly found tenants and buyers for his unconventional apartments in Berlin's Prenzlauer Berg district demonstrates that there is a demand for well-designed, innovative apartment housing – even in this marketplace.

1.1 Women's dormitory in Kumamoto, Kumamoto Prefecture, Japan
   Kazuyo Sejima and Associates 1991

1.2

Housing Construction as a Planning Task
Housing is undoubtedly one of the most exciting tasks for architects. Not least of all because it satisfies basic needs, the most fundamental task of architecture, which has been closely linked to social issues ever since the industrial revolution. All architects have living spaces of their own somewhere and can therefore easily identify with the planning task. On the other hand, high-density housing remains an anonymous field because the future users are rarely known. This is in contradiction to the thesis that the best results are achieved if the building is tailored to the individual needs of the inhabitants. Housing, in particular, is caught in the force field between societal and ecological necessities and user requirements. The fact that the overwhelming majority of the population dream of their own home in the countryside must be harmonized with the necessity for high-density housing in order to halt urban sprawl and prevent further developement of green spaces and the increase in traffic that is associated with it (see pp. 12). Clearly, new concepts are needed.

The buildings featured in this book illustrate a multitude of contemporary solutions for well-designed multi-storey housing. In making the selection, we placed particular value on presenting a broad spectrum of building forms, access situations, floor plans, materials and construction types.

Urban Planning,
Good housing is more than merely the individual building. Traffic links, urban planning accessibility to public facilities, building access as well as the layout and design of green spaces around and between buildings impact the quality of the living space and the social interaction of the inhabitants in fundamental ways. The building itself can become a nucleus for urban infrastructure. With the growing integration of living, work and leisure, there is a need for housing ensembles with facilities that go beyond the mere supply of living space.

Ecology and Building Form
In the interest of resource efficiency, ecological approaches to renovating and increasing the density in the existing fabric should be given preference over new construction. The A/V ratio (ratio of heat-transmitting exterior surface to heated building volume) is a key parameter in choosing the building form. The smaller the surface of the building's envelope that is exposed to the elements, the smaller is the building's heating energy requirement. In addition to building form, the number of floors also plays a key role. High-density housing with apartment towers (of the kind that were built in the 1970s) often create social problems due to the lack of social interaction, the anonymity of their inhospitable access environments and the failure to provide adequate connection to the outdoor space. For this reason the height of most of the examples featured in this book does not exceed five or six storeys. Nevertheless there are interesting approaches even in the high-rise type, as demonstrated by two examples from Japan. While Kazuyo Sejima creates opportunity for social interaction as well as generous private outdoor spaces by means of exterior corridors and two-storey open atria in her housing row, Riken Yamamoto has translated the principle of the residential district into the vertical plane with a system of internal streets in his residential high-rise (see pp. 78 and pp. 82).

Access
Among the many access options, a basic differentiation is made between access provided via stairwells or exterior corridors. Residents will be more receptive to corridors with attractive qualities that render them usable as an extension of the living space. They can be particularly useful in cases where the efficient integration of an elevator is necessary (for example, for wheelchair accessibility). Exterior corridors are also suited for providing access to maisonettes – a building type with two or more floors, which makes it possible to transfer the qualities of the "little house" to multi-storey buildings.

Floor Plan
Floor plans must take the changing social conditions into account and respond to the shift in household configurations, as well as to changes within a family. Fewer and fewer apartments are home to the classic nuclear family and the variety in contemporary lifestyles is reflected in adaptable housing structures. Be it housing co-op, nuclear family or single-parent family, work at home or home office – what is required are flexible apartments where most rooms are usage neutral in plan. Flexibility does not have to mean shifting dividing walls. Thus floor plans with a neutral space at the entrance, which can be used alternatively as a guest room or study, or as a room for an older child or a grandparent, are equally sensible solutions (see pp. 26).

Construction
The examples that follow illustrate that all available primary building materials (wood, steel, masonry and reinforced concrete) are suitable for progressive housing construction. In addition to regional conditions and regulations, design considerations and physical properties, the choices are also based on the ideas and requirements of the users. Building costs are an essential criterion in housing construction, especially in publicly subsidized projects. The choice of a particular material based on cost depends on local circumstances and on availability, as well as on the qualifications of the craftsmen and contractors. The timber construction systems that are standard today are ideal for realizing flexible floor plan solutions; steel- and reinforced steel skeleton construction is equally suitable. Timber construction systems are also interesting from an ecological perspective: these systems almost always achieve low-energy standards and a total energy balance that is hard to beat.

1.3

1.2 Solitary structures in Innsbruck, Baumschlager & Eberle 2000
1.3 Housing ensemble in London, Haworth Tompkins 2002

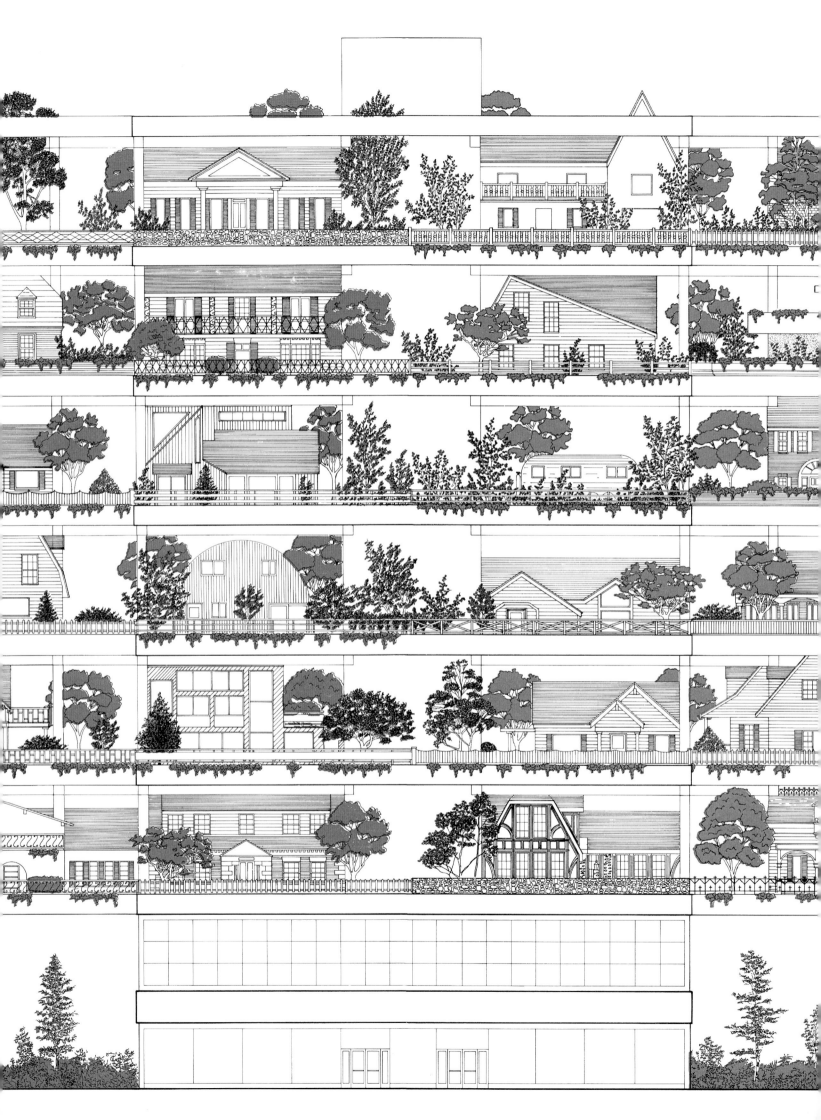

From Isolation in the Peripherie to the Highrise of Homes in the City

Klaus-Dieter Weiß

Every dream of a home begins with the convergence of the desire for individual happiness and the vision of passing on a dream villa on a lake as an inheritance – never with the vision of an apartment in the city. The consequences for the city are devastating: the loss of inhabitants in the long term. The consequences are no less dramatic with regard to innovation in housing construction, for demand is only focused on transitional solutions. Yet the beautiful illusion of the country retreat conceals many hidden problems, even in the ideal case of the villa on a lake. Apart from the fact that the reality of small, prefabricated subdivision homes on small lots far from the city doesn't come anywhere near to the dream, no matter how carefully the running costs may be calculated. These days, the average American spends ten years of his life in the car, because housing no longer takes the needs of urbanity, integration and self-determination into consideration. The thriving trade in books on tape began with bumper-to-bumper traffic in the United States because commuters in that country no longer read books in lawn chairs: all they can do is listen while driving. Even so, stressed-out homeowners and daily commuters are unlikely to analyze the loss of time related to the location of their property. There's simply no time – even for this.

Living in linear housing developments in a so-called green setting has been debunked as individual isolation in an environment that offers neither spatial qualities nor urbanity. In practice, a modest distance of two times three metres between detached homes becomes an inhospitable and labour-intensive nuisance rather than a place of individual freedom. Acoustic screening and independence from neighbours are more effectively achieved with structural noise protection by technical means. When the immediate vicinity is neither visible nor audible, the city apartment integrated into the urban fabric can be far more luxurious than the detached country home, provided both alternatives offer identical, house-like qualities of living: in the interior and at the transition to the appropriate exterior space – a small yard, a winter garden or a (roof-)patio. Unfortunately few apartments in multi-storey dwellings meet this requirement and those that do are generally only in cases where architects plan for themselves. The decision to opt for home ownership beyond the city boundaries, a voluntary choice it would seem, is in truth a flight from the insufficient housing options in the city, and less a rejection of the city as a place to live.

In his poem "Das Ideal"[1], Kurt Tucholsky described the resulting dilemma of individual living in 1927, four years before Le Corbusier offered a concrete proposal in his most spectacular sketch (ill. 2.9), complete with ground plan and section, albeit unfortunately still adhering to the urban planning doctrine of the time without providing the urban integration, which Tucholsky had identified as being necessary:

"ja, das möchste:
Eine Villa im Grünen mit großer Terrasse,
vorn die Ostsee, hinten die Friedrichstraße;
mit schöner Aussicht, ländlich-mondän,
vom Badezimmer ist die Zugspitze zu sehn
aber abends zum Kino hast dus nicht weit.
Das Ganze schlicht, voller Bescheidenheit:
Neun Zimmer, – nein, doch lieber zehn!
Ein Dachgarten, wo die Eichen drauf stehn,
Radio, Zentralheizung, Vakuum,
eine Dienerschaft, gut gezogen und stumm,
eine süße Frau voller Rasse und Verve
(und eine fürs Wochenend, zur Reserve)
eine Bibliothek und drumherum
Einsamkeit und Hummelgesumm.
Im Stall: Zwei Ponies, vier Vollbluthengste,
acht Autos, Motorrad – alles lenkste
natürlich selber – das wär ja gelacht!
Und zwischendurch gehst du auf Hochwildjagd."[1]

Urbanity

Living in the city offers irreplaceable advantages as soon as the variety of urban life is played out within reach right in front of one's own doorstep. City cannot be replaced by suburban periphery or country retreats. Conversely, the quality of living aimed for in the country retreat can easily be surpassed in an urban condominium with the help of architectural and technical means. It also offers the advantage of spending up to ten years of one's life more freely and productively than being tied with both hands to the steering wheel of a car. Over seventy years ago, Le Corbusier created the fundamental basis for living in one's own home and in the city. In his book *"La ville radieuse"*, published in 1935, the revolutionary idea is described in bare words: "Here are 'artificial sites', vertical garden cities. Everything has been gathered here: space, sun, view; means of immediate communication, both vertical and horizontal; (…). The architectural aspect is stunning! The most absolute diversity, within unity. Every architect will build his villa as he likes; what does

2.1 Housing project "Highrise of Homes," S.I.T.E., 1981

it matter to the whole if a Moorish-style villa flanks another in Louis XVIth or in Italian Renaissance? (…) The artificial lots are created first: highway + floorings of the substructure. And these sites are put up for sale as villas with garden and limitless view."[2] The fascination of historic cities lies in their multifaceted spatiality, which did not, by any means, grow without human intervention, but was professionally planned. The individual elements of these urban structures are not diminished by their urban integration – they are enriched by it. It was Le Corbusier, of all people, the modern revolutionary, who wanted to raze the old city to the ground, who projected this motif onto the vertical plane, exponentially increasing the feasibility of single-family homes in high-density housing in the city, at least in theory.

Based on Le Corbusier's idea, projects are currently being realized that once again propagate the social and ecological imperative of returning to the city. The spectrum ranges from the luxurious and wildly ambitious to the realistic and site-related. The Spanish architect Santiago Calatrava is currently planning a 300-m-high apartment tower on the banks of the East River in the South Street Seaport District in downtown Manhattan.[3] The project title "Townhouses in the Sky" summarizes the conceptual idea: twelve glazed cubes of four storeys each, suspended within a filigree concrete core (ill 2.2). Each unit is a modern expression of a four-storey urban townhouse. In other words: a 300-m-tower for twelve luxury homes. The completion is scheduled for 2007. Hadi Teherani from the architectural firm Bothe Richter Teherani (BRT) has chosen an entirely different path. His new programmatic goal is succinctly encapsulated in the abbreviation "home4," another concept that is yet to be realized. Even the project description expands the boundaries into the fourth dimension of living, the time factor. Like Santiago Calatrava, Hadi Teherani pursues the realization of the same old dream: life in a single-family home in the highrises of the city. And like Le Corbusier, Hadi Teherani also aims for proximity to water and a panoramic view. But contrary to the customary dreams and visions for urban design, he keeps his sights firmly fixed on the small-scale and hence more urban reality of the city. In the meantime, this housing model is being translated into concrete form at sites such as the Speicherstadt in Hamburg, a district of old warehouses, or the Rheinauhafen in Cologne (ills. 2.3, 2.4).

The Growing City

Despite dwindling development and demolition plans in economic problem areas in Germany, housing demands are unabated in urban centres such as Munich or Hamburg. Hamburg, in particular, is aiming for considerable population growth from the current 1.7 million to 2 million under the slogan: "Metropolis Hamburg – The Growing City." Hamburg therefore needs housing options that go far beyond mere accommodation, the makeshift solution of apartments. On the other hand, banishing single-family home districts with an almost country flair from the limited urban area of the city-state seems counterproductive in the long term. With a living area of 35.6 m² per resident, the city is second to last in position by comparison to other federal states. Most of the population growth in Hamburg is due to young people: they are open to new ideas and ownership models in housing, whose only commonality with traditional living behind picket fences in the periphery is the two-storeyed structure and the freedom of choice in dividing or organizing the interior. Water, as an element that adds interest, should become a reference

2.2

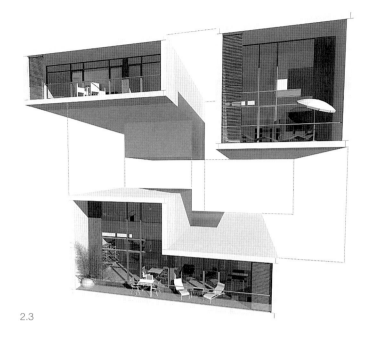

2.3

point for housing in many cities; Hamburg's greatest appeal lies in its new waterfront, the Hafen-City. The concept of "home[4]", tranquil and individual, architecturally appealing "habitation" in a verdant condominium – a synthesis of country villa and city home – is seen as the remedy with the goal of inspiring new enthusiasm for living in the city.

To this day, the dissolution of urban density has failed to produce spatially appealing and socially inspiring solutions. Neither Le Corbusier's city transformed into a park landscape with individual highrises complete with integrated retail strips, nor Ebenezer Howard's garden city movement, launched over a century ago, succeeded in replacing the charm of the real, dynamic and spontaneous city. To exaggerate, one might say that both alternatives were an attempt at urban planning as a surrogate. In one case with the help of free-floating housing steamships, in the other with the help of allotment gardens. The model of the gated community implemented today as part of the new urbanism in the United States is just as hostile to urban living. A review of the history of types and ideas on the house-like city apartment in the "highrise of homes" is therefore vitally important for the debate. What is notable is that nearly every essential feature has been conceived, expressed and drafted since Le Corbusier, particularly in the 1960s and 1970s. With the exception of rare, often long-since forgotten attempts, there is a complete lack of built examples. The genealogy of the "villa in the sky" that follows, presented in a kaleidoscope of utopias, citations, buildings, projects and commentaries, elevates this secondary choice in housing development, so rich in opportunities for future urban development, as the principal theme. It provides a time-lapse review of the evolution thus far and enables us to draw conclusions for the current situation.

Densification

In 1966, the German architect and regional planner Eckhard Schulze-Fielitz, who, like Archigram, Superstudio, Yona Friedman or Kenzo Tango, sought to transform urban design and architecture by means of flexible spatial constructs, explained that densification need not have a negative connotation if it generates synergetic advantages in the urban context: "There seems to be a conviction that densification alone has negative consequences because building regulations place a limit on maximum, but not on minimum density. (…) The legally imposed dilution of use is an expropriation for which there is no compensation, increasing communications costs and the time expended in the use of the city. (…) The districts dating from the late nineteenth century – teething troubles of the first industrial revolution – have encouraged a mode of thinking in urban planning, according to which the best density is avoidance of density in the first place."[4] Urbanity is not merely a product of density – this supposition was, as we now know, a fallacy in the models propagated in the 1960s. The catchy motto at the conference of the Bund Deutscher Architekten (BDA or Association of German Architects) in 1963 – "Society through Density" – was in fact intended as a provocative response to the urban sprawl scenario propagated by the German government. Even then,

2.4

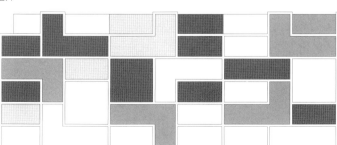

2.2   Housing project "Townhouses in the sky" in New York,
       Santiago Calatrava, completion scheduled for 2007
2.3, 2.4 Housing project "home 4" in Hamburg and Cologne,
       Hadi Teherani, completion scheduled for 2005

Yona Friedmann questioned the causal relationship between society and density and pleaded for a scientific approach to urban planning in imitation of modern physics – not only with regard to the spatial dimension, but also in consideration of the time factor; above all, however, as a departure from urban planning and design founded exclusively in artistic intuition and personal preferences.[5] Conversely, the current goal of creating an ecological city is surely unattainable without densification and re-densification.

Living in a single-family house is not nearly as integrated as the seamless transition between house and garden seems to suggest. On the contrary, living in a single-family house outside of the city is invariably one-dimensional living. It adheres to a purely linear order. It is true that the available outdoor spaces are at ground level and privately owned. But it is impossible to create a spatial context out of the legally imposed dividing strips. The largest section of the garden remains unused, a green space purely for show, a relic of the "elegant villa," while still requiring maintenance and care. The German sociologist Hans-Paul Bahrdt was prompted to comment laconically in 1961: "Suburban houses and single-family homes, set precisely into the centre of very small lots as a result of building regulations, are less responsive to the desire for privacy than apartments." The argument should give us pause: never before have the stages for blissful home ownership on the periphery been as restricted as they are today. Even the Austrian Roland Rainer, one of the most passionate champions of high-density low-rise building, had to admit in 1974: "The desire for privacy, which drives most people to strive towards owning a 'single-family home' at great personal cost and tremendous public expense, is not satisfied by the contemporary form of these houses." In addition to this, the enormous deficiencies of one-dimensional living have to be compensated at the expense of individual time and money in a manner that is questionable, both ecologically and economically. The only alternative is to tolerate them by accepting a complete loss of cultural and social life. The ability to choose freely among several options, on the other hand, is a quality that differentiates life in high-density housing in the city from the supposedly countrified lifestyle in the periphery. The evil spectre of the apartment or "social housing," however, stood in the way of a clear-sighted view of these dynamics. Ulrich Conrads, editor-in-chief of the journal *Bauwelt* for many years, unmasked the comparison of apartment versus house as false and debunked the myth of the majority of single-family homes by comparison to social housing by coining the expression "social houses," an expression that, unfortunately, failed to take hold. The motto of the "Society through Densification" or "Urbanity through Densification" was full of negative connotations by comparison to the garden city idea of the turn of the last century. And yet there was nothing wrong with it. What was wrong across the board was the architectural response – on both sides of the city wall. The slogan: "As many single-family homes as possible, as few rental apartments as possible," was especially wrong. For Le Corbusier's apartment homes had long been forgotten by then.

Integration
The Russian-born Serge Chermayeff, successor of Laszlo Moholy-Nagy at the Institute of Design in Chicago, and the Viennese Christopher Alexander, both trained in England,

composed their remarkable seminal work *Community and privacy: toward a new architecture of humanism* chiefly with a view to integration. This was an idea that was close to Christopher Alexander's heart, among other reasons because he had studied mathematics as well as architecture: "The pseudo country house sits uneasily in its shrunken countryside, neither quite cheek by jowl with its neighbor nor decently remote, its flanks unprotected from prying eyes and penetrating sounds. It is a ridiculous anachronism. (…) The bare unused islands of grass serve only the myth of independence. This unordered space is neither town nor country; behind its romantic façade, suburbia contains neither the natural order of a great estate nor the man-made order of the historic city. (…) The suburb fails to be countryside because it is too dense. It fails to be city because it is not dense enough. Countless scattered houses dropped like stones on neat rows of development lots do not create an order, or generate community. Neighbor remains stranger and the real friends are most often quite far away, as are school, shopping and other facilities. (…) In spite of growing decentralization, and the fact that more and more people with more and more cars live in the never-never land of Suburbia, most of the money continues to be earned and spent in the city proper."[6]
It is remarkable how the arguments put forth in expert circles around the globe converged without having the slightest effect on the practice of urban planning, a few exceptions aside. The practical solution proposed by Chermayeff and Alexander was dense carpet development composed of deep, single-storey buildings set around garden courtyards with a network of narrow, labyrinthine connecting paths closed off to traffic. For the United States, this was a revolutionary, area-efficient approach in the spirit of Roland Rainer, albeit not a constructive, long-term urban strategy by comparison to the far more complex model of the European city. As Lewis Mumford stated, the city is justifiably regarded as "the most precious invention of civilization, second only to language in its role as a mediator of culture."[7] It is the quintessential repository of history. Nevertheless, the last fifty years have been marked by the unfettered sprawl of subdivisions, all driven by the untouchable decree of home ownership. We have forgotten that the city experience begins on the doorstep of one's private home, fundamentally influencing daily life with shopping and leisure, the route to school and office, culture and communication: depending on aesthetic stimuli and the free choice between entering into contact or keeping a distance, this influence is experienced as positive or negative. In their individual districts, large cities should strive to emulate small towns and create a unique space as a focal point, a "small, comfortably everyday public sphere, which has, however, nothing in common with the village linden tree of the pre-industrial village,"[8] as Hans-Paul Bahrdt put it in 1968. Modern apartments in this varied ensemble of functions and forms should not only declare their modernity through advanced technology, but above all by providing their residents with opportunities for cultural growth in the immediate vicinity. Seen from this perspective, the size of a largely autonomous urban quarter is defined by the range one can comfortably cross on foot: ten minutes, that is, 10 000 residents. "The degree of densification," states Bahrdt, "thus determines whether retail stores for daily use, schools, pubs and churches are reachable on foot, whether access by public transport is possible, or, conversely,

whether there is a need for individual transportation, which will, in turn, have consequences for the expansion of the road infrastructure."[9]

Gordon Cullen, the Camillo Sitte of the 1960s, led the debate on this topic in England with his groundbreaking special edition volume *The functional tradition* published by *Architectural Review*.[10] It took thirty years before a German edition of the book, which is out of print today, was published. The limited accessibility of these important sources makes a rigorous continuation of this debate difficult enough to begin with. It seems necessary, therefore, to quote the vital passages of the central positions verbatim: "There are advantages to be gained from the gathering together of people to form a town. A single family living in the country can scarcely hope to drop into a theatre, have a meal out or browse in a library, whereas the same family living in a town can enjoy these amenities. The little money that one family can afford is multiplied by thousands and so a collective amenity is made possible. A city is more than the sum of its inhabitants. It has the power to generate a surplus of amenity, which is one reason why people like to live in communities rather than in isolation. (…) One building standing alone in the countryside is experienced as a work of architecture, but bring half a dozen buildings together and an art other than architecture is made possible. Several things begin to happen in the group which would be impossible for the isolated building. We may walk through and past the buildings, and as a corner is turned an unsuspected building is suddenly revealed. We may be surprised, even astonished (a reaction generated by the composition of the group and not by the individual building). (…) In fact there is an *art of relationship* just as there is an art of architecture. Its purpose is to take all the elements that go to create the environment: buildings, trees, nature, water, traffic (…), and to weave them together in such a way that drama is released. For a city is a dramatic event in the environment."[11] In this passage, Cullen formulated the decisively more complex antithesis to Le Corbusier's definition of "the masterful, correct and magnificent play of masses brought together in light."[12]

The Highrise of Homes
In his housing experiment 'Habitat' at EXPO '67 in Montréal (ill. 2.6), Moshe Safdie demonstrated that the ideal housing form of the future should be sought in a combination of single-family house and apartment. The spectacular, strongly articulated macrostructure of 158 housing units, linked by an elaborate network of bridges and constructed from prefabricated, industrial concrete boxes, which are assembled like Lego building blocks into a honeycombed open housing pyramid, inspired countless utopian projects, but few concrete realizations. The British architects and landscape planners John Darbourne and Geoffrey Darke, on whose work no major publication exists to this day with the exception of a small exhibition catalogue, had already designed a more realistic concept in 1961 with their Lillington Gardens project, a residential complex in London that responds to the city and its spatial requirements, the first building phase of which was completed in 1968 (ill. 2.5). Only in this case, the individual housing unit

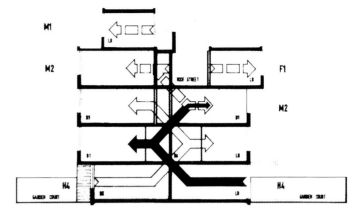

2.5

2.6

2.5 "Lillington Gardens" housing complex in London, Darbourne & Darke, 1972
2.6 "Habitat" housing experiment at EXPO '67 in Montreal, Moshe Safdie, 1967

2.7

2.8

was barely legible from the outside due to a complicated arrangement of living levels, in contrast to Le Corbusier's epochal proposal.

A review of innovation in housing, undertaken in 1987, was thus doomed to reach a negative conclusion: residents are all too ready to interpret the failure of urban housing construction as their own failure in achieving the path toward the ultimate salvation and happiness of their own home – for financial reasons. Any rapprochement between dream and reality in high-density housing is seen as utopian, there is no demand for it and, hence, no supply in keeping with the mechanisms that drive the market. However, a crude strategy of currying favour with the favourite choice of the building savings plan holder would be tantamount to confusing a preference born from a forced decision with a choice between true alternatives. For the public makes a simple choice with regard to accommodation. The less advantageous the stacked goods in mass housing, the more appealing is the lure of habitation on one's own initiative.[13]

According to the liberalism of the Scottish national economist Adam Smith, the free actions of individuals driven by the pursuit of personal advantage are the foundation of all natural and social laws. However, in the context of urban planning the factual renunciation of planning and supervision failed to fulfil the optimistic thesis of an equilibrium based on fulfilment of all individual interests. With the loss of control over the building ground, the public sector also lost all regulatory influence on the real estate market. Thus the history of ideas and initiatives always fell behind the history of trends and facts. While the room to manoeuvre in the interest of personal decisions was limited in the old bourgeois city, there was freedom for individual architectural expression within a prescribed pattern that was accepted as given. Today, the question of how the ill-advised subjects who were to be the masters of the city, live, or rather how they wish to live, remains unanswered. Architectural and urbanistic alternatives, with which the individual could correct his illusions and expand his fantasies, are lacking. In 1971, the architecture critic Wolfgang Pehnt mused: "The fact that we know more about the habitat behaviour of song birds than the habitation behaviour of human beings does not have to remain the status quo." But even this attempt at bringing science to bear in urban planning fell on deaf ears.

Aesthetics

In 1983, when postmodernism was in full swing, the Munich architect and publicist Christoph Hackelsberger stressed the lost opportunities of modular building, which Moshe Safdie had realized in a spectacular singular event without opportunity for continuation after EXPO '67 and which is being newly implemented today in the housing model of "home[4]". Hackelsberger, too, bemoaned the lack of concrete research in housing: "While there were a considerable number of demonstration building measures in the postwar era, there was never any true research of housing in terms of optimizing desirable floor plan solutions and exploring a degree of spatial flexibility by attaching or detaching autonomous areas as

2.7 Urban plan for Nemours/Algeria, Unité d'Habitation, Le Corbusier, 1934
2.8 Terraced maisonette block "Domaine de Badjara" in Algiers, Le Corbusier, 1932
2.9 "Plan Obus," vertical garden city beneath urban highway, Le Corbusier, 1931

well as minimizing the effort. When superficial attention to industrial building became a fashionable trend in the 1970s, people were caught up in what can only be described as a euphoric mood, blinded by the successes of academic architecture. But the first oil crisis put an end to the largely questionable efforts and prompted a detour towards pseudo-craftsmanship and folkloristic approaches. Modular building, which would have had a real chance of improving housing with an abundance of variety and cost-efficiency, fell by the wayside. There was no demand for such things, especially in the building trade and the dominant market forces, which, taking the Neue Heimat as an example, delivered monotonous mass products idealized by architects."[14]

In his search for social imagination in urbanity and community, Sigfried Giedion referred in 1956 to Le Corbusier's Unité d'Habitation in Marseilles, completed four years previously, as stunning proof that housing would in future no longer have to be restricted to "individual housing cells arranged in stacks or rows." The basic idea of expanding the concept of housing, then and now, consists in creating more airy living environments even in the highrise – with the help of two-storey spaces even at the expense of living area. Already in his villa blocks from 1922, an individual unit of which was exhibited in Paris in 1925, Le Corbusier designed apartment living in a house-like manner on two floors, exponentially increasing the possibilities for privacy and space in the apartment type. In Marseille, each two-storey maisonette was, as Giedion stressed, oriented toward two sides: "To the east, the view embraces an arena of limestone mountains in the distance, as they are seen everywhere in Provence. To the west, the view offers the blue expanse of the Mediterranean in the distance and the tranquil aspect of green tree tops nearby, punctuated by red tiled rooftops." The principal shortcoming of this model was the fact that the urban spatial integration of housing with the immediate vicinity had been abandoned in favour of separating functions in the spirit of the Charter of Athens, which was operative at the time. Yet Le Corbusier's housing model would have been ideally suited to the modular demands of a modern building industry.

The housing reform, successful both architecturally and in terms of interior space, which Le Corbusier propagated within the framework of preserving the qualities of an open and flexible floor plan, and which had already been expressed in the anonymous architectural style of the American single-family house even prior to Frank Lloyd Wright, failed to become the standard in the competition for the private detached home – not even with regard to the internal spatial qualities. Whereas the single-family house could claim to be "unique," even in cases where it satisfied only the lowest common denominator of design in the form of vulgar functionalism on a lot of one's own, mass housing on the urban periphery was hit especially hard by the architectonic simplifications of the 1950s, 60s and 70s – further exacerbating the chasm between individual and community, between villa resident and the "average barrack-dwelling Central European." (Roland Rainer) The sociologist Hans-Paul Bahrdt issued an urgent warning against this erroneous development in 1961: "The thoughtless identification of home ownership with low-rise building, on the one hand, and rental accommodation and multi-storey buildings, on the other, is especially fatal."

Mobility

The ultimate dream home, the detached single-family house, quickly turns into a horror image, especially if one takes a close look at the time schedule of its inhabitants: according to current data gathered by the relevant federal ministry in Germany, every driver spends 96 minutes on the road on average per day, covering an average distance of 44 kilometres (driving to work and schools 21%, shopping 19%, errands including "dropping off and picking up" 21%, leisure traffic 31%). The average time effort is therefore 11.2 hours per week, or more than 24 days per year. Based on time calculations practiced by labour unions, this translates into almost seventeen 35-hour weeks. From a purely economic perspective, the work time required to finance private transportation has to be added as well, especially since every household has an average of 1.1 cars (0.8 in 1989), that is, since over 28 per cent of all households run more than one car. According to the ADAC (German automobile association) the total cost of driving a VW Golf, model 1.9 TDI, 44 km/day or 16000 km/year, runs to more than €5000 per year. If this enforced mobility were to be avoided by optimizing access to local facilities and creating more attractive

2.9

living environments in a city "of short paths," urban dwellers would gain as much as two to three months of "available time" per year by comparison to commuters. And this doesn't even take the ecological and overall economic costs into account. The quickest remedy to the purely economic misery of urban sprawl today are commuter ride programs, which aim for a greater number of passengers per car (1.04 for business commuters). On the other hand, this model of everyday group travel is hardly compatible with the dreamed-of individuality associated with living in a single-family house. Germany isn't far behind the dramatic time losses experienced by American commuters. The reversal of this trend, both politically and in terms of urban planning, is becoming ever more difficult.

But even this thesis is nothing new, as a prominent example illustrates. In the United States, Victor Gruen, born in Vienna in 1903, is widely regarded as the father of the shopping mall and – later on – of the urban pedestrian zone. His plea for a humane-ecological approach to urban planning, released in 1975, is therefore also rooted in his own errors: "The tragicomic aspect of the worship of mobility is that the era of the highest point in the civilization of humankind began when man settled down, when he abandoned his nomadic life and his occupation of hunting and gathering and turned to cultivation, crafts, commerce and trade. (…) The settled way of life gave rise to the virtues of *civitas* or to that which we call civilization thanks to law, art and science. The only remarkable thing is that after some 10 000 years of practicing a settled way of life, humankind has returned to a nomadic lifestyle. (…) As a result we expend so much time and energy for our vagabond existence, that we have very few means and possibilities at our disposal for the provision of our houses and apartments, our neighborhoods and cities. (…) How can we plan cities so that the distances will be as short as possible and the quality of all the space where we take shelter, that is the homes, and the quality of the compulsory spaces, that is the workplaces, and, finally, the quality of the elective space, these are the theatres, cinemas, discotheques, etc., is so extraordinary that our homes, as the principal element, are characterized by such a superior 'diverting' quality that we will choose to spend most of our time there and not feel the need to seek other places. (…) If I were to pose the question whether the quality of living, which I experienced up to 1938 in a relatively modest rental apartment (in downtown Vienna) was worse than the quality of living, which I now enjoy in a luxurious house (complete with four cars) in one of the best suburbs of Los Angeles (25 km from downtown), I would have to answer in the negative."[15]

Individuality

Thirty years ago, Roland Rainer, the prominent champion of high-density, low-rise building, was also fascinated by the alternative, more urban idea of single-family homes in condominiums: "In view of the desolate banality of most rental apartments, erected today by various developers, on the one hand, (…) in view of the well-documented rapid change in family dynamics, lifestyles and living standards, on the other hand, the idea of being able to buy or rent a floor, where one could create living spaces with adjacent patios etc. to one's own specifications and connect them to cables of all kinds, thus gaining an individual home, a single-family house in the air, so to speak, without land use, access costs or garden

2.10

'work,' has tremendous appeal."[16] Le Corbusier created his stunning sketch of this dream seventy years ago as part of his urban planning study for Algiers (ill. 2.9). In the impressive Gesamtkunstwerk, which caused quite a stir, it is above all this small drawing, which became one of the architect's most published works. This was only after 1961, however, when the Dutchman Nicolaas John Habraken found inspiration in it for his book *Supports: an alternative to mass housing* – albeit without any specific reference to the connection. The English edition of the book was published in 1972, the German edition only in 2000. In 1970, Le Corbusier's sketch had been published in the Netherlands on an enormously large scale of nearly one metre in length, together with a contribution to housing construction. Although sections and plans have survived, neither Le Corbusier's sketch nor Habraken's book were aimed at concrete realization: their impact lay chiefly in the suggestive effect they had.

Attempts at stacking the status symbol of the villa in its antiquated image value must be seen as pure utopia. One illusory draft, which the American group of architects S.I.T.E. adopted from a then more than seventy-year-old illustration in *Life* magazine in 1981 to inspire enthusiasm for a revised edition under the title "Highrise of Homes" in Manhattan, at the site, no less, of New York's Modern Museum of Art, has failed to contribute any built projects to this day. The airspace above the double roof of the homes offers no advantage whatsoever, does not reveal the sky but only an inescapably banal view of the underside of the ceiling. Both drawings, which should be rated rather as caricatures, – dating from 1909 and 1981, respectively – simply prove how deeply the image of the villa is rooted in pure status value beyond any form of practical utility (ill. 2.1). Nevertheless, the idea is so striking that it is little wonder that it was unable to establish itself. The only project of this kind realized thus far, by Erik Friberger in Göteborg, failed to draw any attention: a total of no less than eighteen single-family homes were realized as early as 1960 on vertically stacked concrete foundations.[17] The goal, as valid as ever, has led to a building in Göteborg, which delivers the antithesis to the theoretically logical chain of argumentation in a crowning conclusion. Given the banality of a parking garage structure with awkwardly placed single-family homes, almost like mass housing in type, architecture is increasingly diminished to the level of technical administration of individual interests. Following the failure of their luxury condominiums in practice, the S.I.T.E. group quickly drew the appropriate conclusion and offered an economy model. It makes do without any individually formulated roofs, displaying only a few superficial ornamentations and props attached to a fixed building structure that is wholly adapted to the usual stacked mass housing: turrets, gables, facades with seemingly rich variations, fronting standardized, narrow plans. The row of wall-to-wall catalogue houses leaves only one facade free in the planned "theatre." According to the script, it too is forced to act the part of a house – complete with front door, doorbell and front yard. Functionally, however, this is the garden side with the only available open space. The real access paths run along the rear – just as wretched as those in Göteborg.

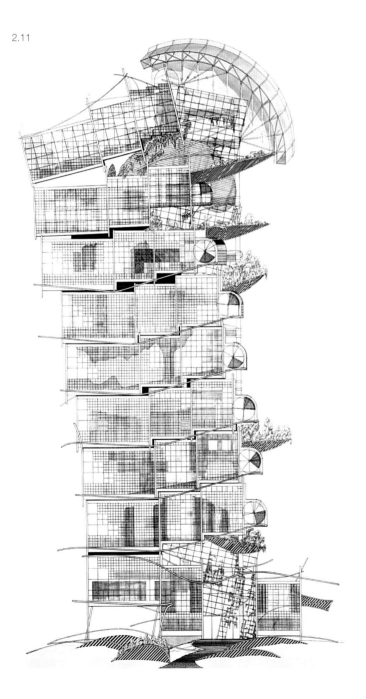

2.11

2.10 Design sketch for Löwengasse housing complex in Vienna, Friedensreich Hundertwasser, 1984

2.11 Design for a studio tower in Frankfurt-Sachsenhausen, Peter Cook 1984

It would make more sense to combine the modular building blocks, which Moshe Safdie had already used like Lego bricks to multiply the spatial options available to the residents, with an individual facade section in the overall elevation of the building. Identification by colour alone – as in Le Corbusier's loggias fronting his Unités d'Habitation – is too little, however. Only a structured city is a recognizable city. This task is made easier by the fact that the demand for individual appearance and the necessity of outdoor space as a garden experience on each level overlap in the exterior view of the condominium. Each unit is indispensably reliant on immediate contact with nature, that is, on an encounter with biological processes. As the Swiss architect Otti Gmür illustrated in 1977, the space required to meet this fundamental need is minute: "But earth, water and air must be available to us for this purpose. For the experiences and observations must be made on one's own initiative; in a piece of nature that is more than an attempt to decorate a sterile environment."[18]

Structure
The Dutchman Nicolaas John Habraken caused a sensation with his book, even though it did not contain a single illustration, nor a reproduction of Le Corbusier's sketch. On a purely theoretical level, Habraken pleaded in favour of maintaining the medieval, individual structural principle of the bourgeois home in housing development, even in the big city: "In a really modern town one would have expected an infinitely complex and refined structure, composed of far more cells than the old town. This organism would thus be a unique phenomenon, the cells forming organs and groupings appro-

priate to a very large town, just as in nature highly complicated beings develop more than one organ. The large, but structurally extremely primitive, towns we build now are in total conflict with a society which is developing into an increasingly complex entity with more and more organs, all, however, *composed of the same cells as those in the past!* The demand that the natural relationship be reintroduced is nothing but an inevitable desire to make town structure conform to that of society; the desire to reach in a metropolis the structural harmony between matter and population found only in smaller towns of the past."[19] In an article, he declared: "(…) There is architecture that is uniform and [architecture] that is varied. The latter is based on the principle of 'support and prefabricated elements.' The form of the facade can be so strong that anything is possible within it, without creating a chaotic overall aspect from the outside. This will be experienced as cheerful variety."[20]
Even if the goal for the condominium is simply to achieve greater internal spatial quality and flexibility, which is last but not least also expressed in the external individuality derived from it, the overall aesthetic and spatial expression of the "highrise of homes" must be able to react freely both in scale and in terms of the site, so that the urban space, which is the definitive factor in the value of the housing, is improved rather than compromised. Skyscrapers or horizontal mammoth buildings will rarely be useful additions to an urban inventory. Every new project in the city must be subordinate to the order of the existing configuration and its shape must answer formally to the established spatial parameters. For, according to the theses of the 1970s, it is only the contextual order of the open spaces that creates the site for a building, from which it

2.12

can then develop its own specific, architectural quality. Giving form to publicly accessible open spaces as a sequence of spatial experiences is a central task of urban design. The greater the mix of lifestyles, the more varied and greater is the number of possible experiences and, naturally, also the number of pedestrians. Only a broad spatial spectrum for individual activities, for information, leisure and relaxation, for learning and entertainment, for contemplation and exploration can provide the basis for an atmosphere where the urban dweller is liberated to enter into contact with and encounter those around him. "Architecture is the art of creating public spaces, even in areas where it only realizes private buildings," according to a recent statement by Bazon Brock, the pugnacious professor of aesthetics and cultural critic. How should one judge the spatial standard of the beloved single-family house ghettoes according to this statement? Twenty years ago, Christoph Hackelsberger offered advice on reversing the trend that was as urgent as it was practical: "If we want to reclaim the city in its true function as a driving force of civilization, then we must find our way back to the integration of urban life and activity, evolved over long periods of time, by implementing small, proportionate and intelligent corrections. This rediscovery is only possible by progressing forward." The model of vertical housing construction in the city offers the opportunity for rediscovering civilized urbanity, for the priority of city-creating community. This would create an unexpected, new moment of democratic structuring between the asocial suburbs, the ennui of modern neighbourhoods and the city built around bottom-dollar department stores: each housing unit in the city as an architecturally defined public of the *res publica.* No step toward a revival of the diversity of the city would be more daring than abandoning the endless repetition of housing, and reversing the trend of exiling the citizen from urban traditions. In 1971, Jacob Berend Bakema posed the thought-provoking question: "If our cities were to be buried in ash as Pompeii was all those years ago – what would the archaeologist think upon discovering the endless repetition of identical housing units beneath the ash? Would he recognize it as the expression of a living democracy or of a slave state?"[21]
The urban citizens of the twentieth century were adept at describing in great detail how to positively influence the progress of urban living and of the city. But it is up to the urban dwellers of the twenty-first century to translate the idea into reality.

Intricacy

When Gordon Cullen introduced the concept of intricacy in his book *Townscape,* he coined the definitive expression for the future of housing or building in general in the city: "Intricacy. This quality is perhaps the least understood (or the least demonstrated) in present day building, which seems to stop dead at the obvious, the slab block, the gridiron of curtain walling, the banality of pastel-shaded surfaces giggling down from the sky. But the quality of intricacy absorbs the eye. It is an extra dimension obtained through the knowledge and experience of true professionalism as opposed to the crudities of the amateur."[22] Neither Le Corbusier's plans for Algiers, nor Moshe Safdie's model project Habitat achieved this intricacy, and the utopian images of a "highrise of

2.13

2.12 Client determined building project in Denmark, Susanne Ussing and
       Carsten Hoff 1973
2.13 Caricature of townhouse in the sky, circa 1920

homes" by the American team S.I.T.E. even less so. Will this intricacy become reality through the current concept "home[4]" by Hadi Teherani?

Within the genealogy of the highrise of homes, the distinctive feature of the "home[4]" model lies in the complexity and individuality of the meandering facade exterior, which reflects the broad spectrum of the different one- or multi-storey housing units with flexible internal divisions. At the same time, the labyrinthine motif of this three-dimensional housing puzzle, conceived to be realized at standard market prices, indicates the goal – in contrast to Le Corbusier's visions – of harmonizing the scale with the framework of the existing city. The drafts available thus far present only model solutions. The concept of "home[4]" does not aim to revolutionize the urban space, but to close and complete it. In contrast to all utopian housing hills, funnel- or sprawling cities, this concept demands unambiguous, space-forming geometries. The only prerequisite for the variety is that the individual puzzle pieces must combine into a geometric shape without gaps. The new presence of the "bourgeois home" in the city, which amounts to a renewed shift from "country dweller" to "city dweller," will no doubt have a profound and complex impact on the quality of the city. Recognizing the time-saving of this type of housing in attractive urban settings by comparison to living completely outside of the urban context will accelerate the positive development of a migration into attractive cities.

Incidentally, the advantage of taking a scientific approach also has also been proven in architecture. As early as 1971, Eckehard Schultze-Fielitz already identified the following undeniable advantages resulting from filling neutral systems in a flexible manner:

· Competition among different fill-in methods and systems
· Greater influence of inhabitant on layout and design of his/her private sphere
· Identification of inhabitant with his/her environment
· Artistic freedom
· Units that are distinguishable and hence new materialized, visualized concepts of ownership beyond the currently available, purely legal, condominium ownership
· Subsequent changes (conversion)[23]

The future of living in the city might thus finally gain a new dynamic energy and quality.

2.14

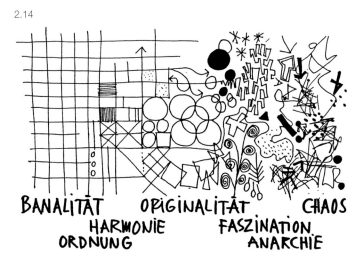

BANALITÄT   ORIGINALITÄT   CHAOS
   HARMONIE   FASZINATION
ORDNUNG   ANARCHIE

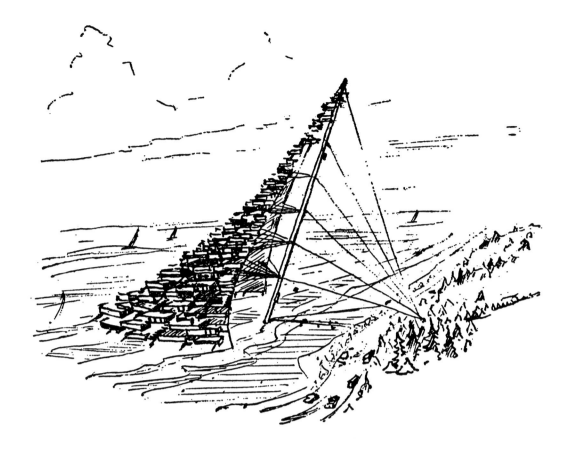

2.15

Notes
1 Kurt Tucholsky, "Das Ideal", Berliner Illustrirte Zeitung, July 31, 1927; [Translation: Here's the perfect setting: / A villa with large terrace in the country, / The Baltic out front and the Friedrichstraße out back; / A beautiful view, fashionably rustic, / With a glimpse of the Zugspitze from your bathroom / But only a short walk to the movies at night. / All of it simple, and oh so modest: / Nine rooms – no, make that ten! / A roof patio with oak trees standing tall, / Radio, central heating, vacuum cleaner, / Servants, obedient and silent, / A sweet wife, full of spirit and passion / (and another for weekends, just in case) / A library and all around / Solitude and bumble bees buzzing. / In the stables: two ponies, four thoroughbreds, / Eight cars, a motorcycle – with you at the wheel, / Of course – that goes without saying! / And in between you go hunting big game.]
2 Le Corbusier, The Radiant City, (New York: The Orion Press, 1967), transl. Eleanor Levieux (Parts II, VI), p. 247
3 Architectural Record, 4/2004, p. 42
4 Eckhard Schulze-Fielitz, Stadtsysteme I, (Stuttgart, 1971), p. 27
5 cf. Gerhard Boeddinghaus (ed.), "Gesellschaft durch Dichte. Kritische Initiativen zu einem neuen Leitbild für Planung und Städtebau 1963/1964," in: Bauwelt Fundamente 107 (Braunschweig, Wiesbaden, 1995)
6 Serge Chermayeff, Christopher Alexander, Community and Privacy. Toward a New Architecture of Humanism. (New York: Anchor Books, Doubleday, 1963), pp. 62
7 Lewis Mumford: Die Stadt. Geschichte und Ausblick (1961), zit. nach: Alexander Mitscherlich: Drei Aspekte der Stadtriesen: Wachstum, Planung, Chaos. In: Uwe Schultz (ed.): Umwelt aus Beton oder Unsere unmenschlichen Städte, (Reinbek 1971), p. 132
8 Hans-Paul Bahrdt: Humaner Städtebau (1968), (Hamburg 1971), p. 118
9 Hans-Paul Bahrdt, op. cit., p. 63
10 The special issue "The functional tradition" published by Architectural Review was followed by a series of articles entitled "Townscape" over nine years and, finally, in 1961 the book of the same title: Gordon Cullen: The Concise Townscape. (London: The Architectural Press, 1961), pp. 7 and 8
11 Gordon Cullen: The Concise Townscape. (London: The Architectural Press, 1961), pp. 6
12 Le Corbusier, Towards a New Architecture, trans. John Rodker, in: Essential Le Corbusier L'Esprit Nouveau Articles (Oxford: Architectural Press, 1998) pp. 29, 131
13 cf. Fischer, Fromm, Gruber, Kähler, Weiß: "Abschied von der Postmoderne," in: Bauwelt Fundamente 64, (Braunschweig, 1987), pp. 103 and 106
14 Christoph Hackelsberger, "Plädoyer für eine Befreiung des Wohnens aus den Zwängen sinnloser Perfektion," in: Bauwelt Fundamente 68, (Braunschweig, 1983)
15 Victor Gruen, Die lebenswerte Stadt, (Munich, 1975), pp. 33/12–13/158
16 Roland Rainer: Für eine lebensgerechtere Stadt (1974), p. 50 Cited in: Gerd Albers, Alexander Papageorgiou-Venetas: Stadtplanung. Entwicklungslinien 1945–1980 (vol. 2), (Tübingen 1984), p. 483
17 cf. Klaus-Dieter Weiß: "Highrise in Göteborg. Etagengrundstücke, Deutsche Bauzeitung 8/1990," in: Wilfried Dechau (ed.): … in die Jahre gekommen. Wohnungsbauten von gestern heute gesehen, (Stuttgart, 1996), pp. 62
18 Otti Gmür: Stadt als Heimat (1977), p. 91. Cited in: Gerd Albers, Op. cit., p. 485
19 Nicolaas John Habraken, SUPPORTS: an alternative to mass housing. Translated from the Dutch by B. Valkenburg Ariba, (London: The Architectural Press, 1972), p. 55
20 TABK-Kath. Bouwblad, (Journal), 1967, p. 385
21 Jacob Berend Bakema: Identität und Intimität der Großstadt, Bauen + Wohnen 1/1964 quote from: Josef Lehmbrock, Wend Fischer: Profitopolis oder: Der Mensch braucht eine andere Stadt, Ausstellungskatalog, Munich 1971, table 4 (o.S.)
22 Gordon Cullen: The Concise Townscape. (London: The Architectural Press, 1961), p. 65
23 Eckhard Schulze-Fielitz, Stadtsysteme I, (Stuttgart, 1971), pp. 57–59

2.14 Study on the aesthetics of neutral structure and individual completion, Eckhard Schulze-Fielitz, 1971
2.15 Project for a "Highrise of Homes" on the beach, Frei Otto, circa 1960

Inside and Outside – The Search for Special Qualities in Contemporary Housing

Eberhard Wurst

"In a house without a bed, the rug that provides cover at night is precious, in the wagon without upholstery the pillow tossed on the hard floor is precious. But in our well-appointed homes there is no place for anything precious because there is no room for the service it can give."[1]
Walter Benjamin

Individualization and Market Constraints

Despite heroic efforts, even the worst shortcomings in housing supply could not be satisfied in the 1920s. At the CIAM congress, convened in Frankfurt in 1929, the modern architecture movement tried to address the housing problem affecting broad sectors of the population. Under the motto "An apartment for the minimum existential requirements" ground plans from all across Europe were shown, which envisioned barely more than 10 m² living area per person.[2] Mies van der Rohe had already opened up new perspectives for modern apartment living in the context of the Werkbund exhibition "Die Wohnung" ("The Apartment") with his contribution of a multi-family house in Stuttgart's Weissenhofsiedlung. On the one hand, he placed great value on rationalization and typification; on the other hand, he commented in his contribution to the exhibition catalogue: "The constantly growing diversity of our housing needs, on the other hand, demands great flexibility in the use of the accommodation. (…) If the architect limits himself to treating the kitchen and the bathroom as constants, because of their plumbing, while partitioning the remaining living area with movable walls, I believe that by these means it is possible to satisfy every reasonable dwelling need."[3]
In Stuttgart, Mies van der Rohe set out to demonstrate the range of possibilities by enlisting twenty-nine architects and interior decorators to design the interiors. The architects – working individually or in teams – designed the floor plan divisions and the furnishings[4] (ill. 3.2). This project successfully illustrated the potential for variability, in part because the architects responded to Mies' vision of creating plans for different groups of residents. Thus a collective of Swiss Werkbund architects, to name but one example, planned a 75 m² apartment for a family of six, with three bedrooms for two beds each based on the cabin principle. A 48 m² apartment was furnished for a family with one child, while a bachelor apartment with the same amount of living space was set up on the floor above.[5] Another apartment was designed for a professional woman – a very progressive idea at the time.[6]

By this means, Mies van Rohe was able to convincingly demonstrate the flexibility of his steel skeleton structure. In giving consideration to different usage options, the criteria for objectively established minimum standards vanished into thin air in his housing block. Gert Kähler comments: "In accordance with the open plan as the architectural image of social emancipation, the architect realized this plan not only in the villa or the purpose-free exhibition pavilion; rather he applied it to mass housing. The fundamentally identical architecture both for the villa of the rich and for the apartment for the masses illustrates the emancipatory claim of the latter."[7]
Far ahead of its time, Mies' concept of housing forms beyond the parent-child(ren)-family foreshadowed today's dynamics. In the mid 1920s there was still very little demand for his idea. But the housing question – a problem seemingly related to quantity alone – was addressed decades later with typified and standardised apartments. In 1995, at the height of the post-reunification boom, more than 600 000 apartments were built in Germany in the space of a single year – six years later, the number dropped to less than half.[8] This comparative lull in construction is taking place today against the background of drastically different social conditions. In 2002, only 30 per cent of the German population lived in households of three or more people (ill. 3.4). The reasons for the continual reduction in the average household size (currently 2.14 people)[9] are complex: the increase in the average age, complex requirements with regard to work planning (flexibility, mobility) and the dissolution of social patterns (gender roles, high divorce rates, migration) bring about a fundamental change in our ways of co-habitation and living.
As household and family constellations become more differentiated, the demands on housing and the housing environment have undergone a complete transformation. Although increasingly at odds with the statistical norm, the motif of family-appropriate accommodation continues to dominate the housing market. Yet the market place has little to offer for many types of households. "Empty nest" and "living apart together" are only two examples, which contribute to the further increase of the average living area, currently at roughly 40 m² per person. This is not to say that greater diversity in terms of lifestyles can only be satisfied

3.1 Housing block in Innsbruck, Georg Driendl 2003

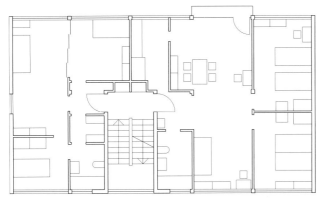

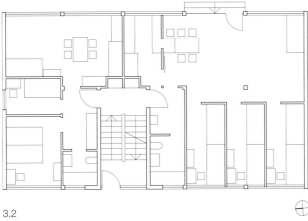

3.2

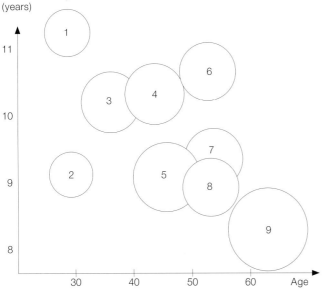

3.3
Post-secondary education
(years)

1	Self-determination type at work and in leisure	9 %
2	Entertainment-/active type	6 %
3	General interest type	12 %
4	Factual, quality-oriented type	12 %
5	Domestic, work-oriented type	13 %
6	Culturally sophisticated/intellectual type	11 %
7	Family-oriented entertainment type	10 %
8	Traditional integration type	11 %
9	Passive, withdrawn type	16 %

with tailor-made floor plans. On the contrary: fragmented housing demands are better served by apartments that respond to changing requirements. Sociologists have recognized this problem and focused on studying so-called "lifestyle concepts" for some time. In addition to conventional models of class and social stratum, these studies classify population according to education, age, leisure patterns, cultural preferences, life goals and everyday behaviour[10] (ill. 3.3).

A close study of individual lifestyle groups does indeed lead to conclusions for housing and living concepts targeted at specific demographics. With only 23 per cent, for example, the "self-determination type at work and in leisure" falls below the average in terms of living in a single-family house, although the desire for such a living arrangement is especially strong among this group, far above average at 79 per cent. The combination of identified shortcomings in available housing development and the high quotient of mobility in this lifestyle group lead to the conclusion that immediate action is required. To keep this affluent and educated clientele in the city, we need living space with single-home qualities. Noise protection, flexible completion options, patios or yards, separate entrances and the latest in technology are listed as important design criteria. "Privacy, presentation or representation are especially important for this type. This group is therefore at the centre of the debate on gentrification and suburbanization."[11]

In Germany, the demand for homeownership is widespread. This is not least of all due to irrefutable facts such as the greater living area, which is 120 m^2 and more in 41 per cent of condominiums as compared to only 5 per cent of rental apartments of a similar size.[12] These facts are complemented by less tangible promises of domestic happiness and a solid base for a stable family life. Mullion and transom windows and folding shutters, elements thought to convey a sense of "freedom and comfort," are listed at the very top in market surveys on client wishes commissioned by the real estate industry. At the same time, high-density housing has met with sharp criticism – even projects that have been recognized with architecture awards.[13] It is no coincidence that the nostalgic architecture of Rob Krier, for example, resonates with many contemporaries. In brand-new developments laid out on a small-town plan, pseudohistoric architectural set pieces are springing up like mushrooms and are highly sought after, not only in the Netherlands (ill. 3.4).

Today, the yearning for "freedom and comfort" is merging with a need for safety, which is satisfied in the so-called gated communities: fenced-in residential developments with security patrols. The presence of a doorman or gatekeeper at the entrance to such housing complexes communicates a sense of certainty that one is leaving the vicissitudes and affronts of the real world behind upon stepping into the building. Alarm systems, and the methods of intruders too, are becoming ever more sophisticated. Styles of fortification, little known in Central Europe for a long time, are changing the urban fabric. A growing trend toward privatizing public space documents social segregation and a rejection of social solidarity at the urban planning level.

New, exclusive "products" are thrown on the market in hitherto unusual combinations to attract an affluent clientele. In addition to golf, tennis and horseback riding facilities, the gentrified residential development is stamped out of the ground as quickly as possible. Cost-to-service ratios or floor plans play only subordinate roles in the thinking that goes into such purchases. The success of these projects is entirely image based. Architectural or even urban planning criteria are delegated to the background. Meanwhile, the justified housing dreams of growing sectors in society still go unanswered.

The decline in subsidized housing over the past twenty years has reduced overall housing construction to a pure investment process or pushed it into niche-markets for subsidized special housing. Switzerland is a notable exception: by comparison to other European countries, it boasts a staggering number of multi-family dwellings combined with a traditionally low ratio of home ownership.[14] Planners in Zurich recognized that the most common housing category in the city, the three- to four-room apartment dating from the 1930s and 40s with an approximate living area of 70 m², can no longer keep up with the growing demands of households with more than two people. Only 8 per cent of all apartments have five or more rooms. A decision was taken in 1998 to counteract the resulting migration of families to the surrounding areas by initiating a program of building "10000 apartments in 10 years." To this end, architecture competitions have been launched, and urban building lots have been made available for co-op housing construction and the conversion of obsolete factory districts (pp. 46, pp. 142). All these projects create high-quality living space that has little in common with the norm that was cultivated for many decades.[15] Other Swiss cities such as Berne and Basel are implementing similar programs.[16] The Dutch Vinex program promotes the construction of family-friendly housing – chiefly townhouses – with similar goals. Currently a total of 750000 townhouses are being constructed at ten locations determined by the state with good linkages to the existing infrastructure. Such targeted interventions in the housing market are the prerequisite for the creation of outstanding projects that overcome imagined as well as real market constraints and help to prevent suburban sprawl.

By comparison to the small, suburban single-family home, high-density housing offers a number of advantages:
• Central location in the city, good connection to public transportation, short distances to school, workplace, etc..
• Good communication with neighbours.
• In tall buildings: apartments with a view.
• Elaborate building systems technology, which is only economically viable when shared between many households.
• Amenities such as sauna, pool and guest apartments.
• Good protection against intruders.
• Decreased property costs as a result of cost-sharing among several units.

In the following paragraphs, the discussion focuses on specific aspects that breathe new life into the idea of high-density housing, by citing contemporary housing examples. Many of these aspects are hardly new; on the contrary, they were first explored many decades ago.

3.4

3.2 Multi-family house Am Weißenhof 14–20 in Stuttgart, Mies van der Rohe, 1927, floor plans for ground floor and 3rd floor, scale 1:200
3.3 Lifestyles in West Germany
3.4 Housing row in the small town of Brandevoort/the Netherlands, under development since 1998, Rob Krier and Christoph Kohl (urban planning)

Changes in Housing Functions

An excellent approach to studying the changes in housing is to take a look at the new requirements for the individual functional areas.

Cooking
The zone for cooking, dining and living offers an especially vivid illustration of the changes and the dissolution of the family unit. Meals are increasingly taken outside of the home, and meal preparation has become nearly obsolete as a result of ready-to-serve meals. "Cooking with fresh ingredients (…) has become a hobby rather than a daily practice for many. Since both forms of cooking are often practiced alternatively in one and the same household, kitchens have to be equipped for all eventualities."[17] The kitchen is also the place where "friends are entertained, children are raised, this is where the mobile family gets together, if they still get together at all. The kitchen is no longer the 'workplace of the house-wife,' but a multi-use, social space that assumes the functions of the living room... It opens onto the outside world in a variety of ways: to the backyard, the winter garden, the neighbourhood."[18]

Living and Dining
Given the changes in the cooking-dining area, the living room has also taken on a different status. The life of adults and children is marked by a growing independence and differences in daily routines. As the individual members of households become more autonomous, floor plan requirements are approaching those of a classic housing co-op. A mere ten years ago, the location of the television was still a reason for shared use of the living room; today, each individual room often features a complete range of media and the living room is no longer the centre of an increasingly fragmented family life. Instead its existence is motivated by a need for representation, much like the "cold splendour" of the bourgeois home in the late nineteenth century.

Individual Rooms/Bedrooms
Up to twenty years ago, most children's rooms were furnished with two beds. Today one bedroom per person is the norm. Raised expectations for withdrawing to a private space have transformed it from the original small sleeping cabin that we know from social housing schemes into a multifunctional living, sleeping and working space. This is where hobbies are pursued and guests are accommodated when the need arises. The various requirements impose a usage-neutral quality on the individual room, which goes hand in hand with a certain minimal size. In order to be able to furnish a room with a double bed, single beds or as a living area, one needs an area of at least 14 m².
Today, however, larger (bed-)rooms no longer translate automatically into smaller living- and dining rooms, as was the case in social housing in the past. Instead, the average rental apartment in Germany has grown from 63 to 68 m² between 1972 and 1993, and the average condominium has increased even more, from an average of 95 to 113 m².[19]
This is all the more astonishing when one considers that the average number of persons per household has decreased drastically over the same period of time.
At first glance, the 3-room apartments in a residential row in Coburg, designed by Fink and Jocher (ill. 3.5), with a net

area of nearly 65 m² are reminiscent of floor plans for steam-ship cabins in the 1920s – still one of the most radical approaches to rationalizing basic living functions. However, whereas Otto Haesler's projects housed[20] two people in a sleeping cell of maximum 9 m², the rooms in the Coburg housing complex are approximately 15 m². A continuous centre-to-centre distance of 3.2 m speaks of a conscious choice to forego specializing the use of these individual rooms in favour of flexibility. Many daily activities of living, which used to take place exclusively in the common area provided in the functional floor plans of the past for reasons of lack of space, have shifted to the private, withdrawing spaces of today. In Coburg, sliding doors expand the rooms into a south-facing "play area," which can be trans-formed into a loggia in summer with the help of foldable wings.

Bathroom
The status of the bathroom has also undergone a transfor-mation. In the 1950s and 60s, mechanical ventilation and extraction created the prerequisites for sanitary modules located in the core, which were integrated into the smallest possible spaces from that time onward. In recent years, by contrast, the bathroom has once again expanded: the space for personal hygiene, its direct lighting, size and fixtures, have become an important yardsticks by which the quality of apartments are assessed. Today a large, well-lit spa bath-room tops the wish list of influential groups of buyers.[21]
The standard dimensions of 4 to 6 m² have been expanded in response to the wish for a double sink, a tub in the middle of the room and a separate shower. The completion standard for a family apartment – one bathroom with tub, sink and WC, as well as guest bathroom with WC at the entrance –, which was the norm for so long, has become superannuated. Recently, many apartments are built with two, fully equipped bathrooms. In an apartment building in Zurich, the architects Birchmeier and Kaufmann take it even one step further: adopting the style of North American single-family houses, they offer ensuite bathrooms for one or two bedrooms (ill. 3.6). Corresponding to its location in the floor plan, the space is thus transformed into the most intimate area of the apartment, creating the prerequisite for combination with the bedroom into a "cocooning-wellness-zone."[22]
The smaller bathroom accessible from the hallway serves for the remaining rooms and as a guest WC.[23]

Working
We are just beginning to decipher the consequences for our work- and living environments resulting from changes in work and providing low-emission and -immission services. With the expansion of information and data-transfer networks, the prerequisites for further growth in telework from home are already in place. Telephone and Internet access in each room has become the norm. In the New York exhibition

3.5 Residential building in Coburg, Fink + Jocher, 1999, standard floor plan, scale 1:200
3.6 Residential building on Breitensteinstrasse in Zurich, Birchmeier Kaufmann, 2002, standard floor plan, scale 1:500
3.7 Kronsbergkarree housing complex in Hanover, Fink + Jocher, 1999, floor plans, scale 1:500, basic structure and optional completion
3.8 The "Vordere Lorraine" residential building in Berne, study group AGW in collaboration with Reinhard + Partner, 2001, floor plans for 3rd and 4th floor, scale 1:500

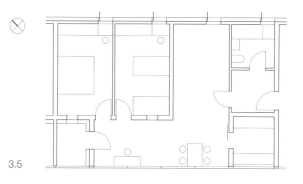

3.5

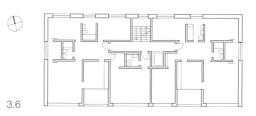

3.6

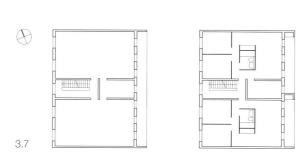

3.7

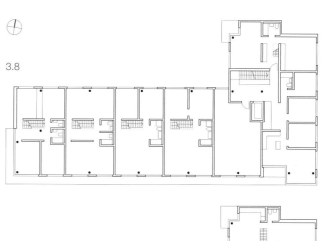

3.8

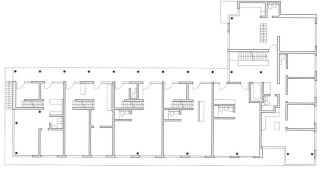

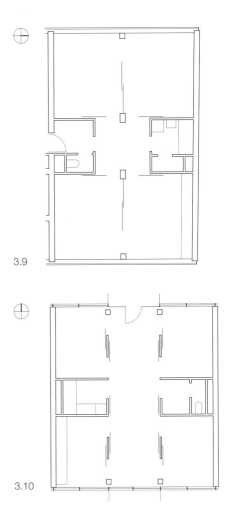

3.9

3.10

3.11

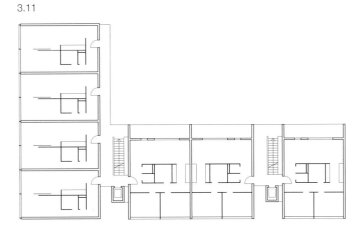

"The un-private house" (1999), Terence Riley described the modern apartment where data reception and transmission is available 24/7, as a "permeable structure." It remains to be seen whether and to which degree increased demands for privacy and retreat are compatible with constant communication, picture telephones and video conferencing. Soon being out of reach will be seen as real quality of life, creating a demand for luxury apartments with screened-off "non-communication zones."

Flexibility

Adapting the apartment to individual needs by simple means is a major topic in housing since the quantitative aspect of the housing question seems to have been solved. Flexibility has long since ceased to be associated with the economy of day-to-night adaptability, which Le Corbusier envisioned with his "Maison Locheur" in 1929, for example. Mies van der Rohe's idea of adaptable building structures from the 1920s is better suited to meeting the needs of changing family scenarios.
Reminiscent of the model housing block in the Weissenhofsiedlung, the architects Fink and Jocher designed a neutral structure for the Kronsberg complex in Hanover which can be divided into various zones (ill. 3.7, see also p. 136).
The centre-to-centre distance of 6 metres is suitable for any floor plan variation from the conventional plans divided into individual rooms with a central corridor, to open living concepts and so-called loft styles. The total depth of 12 metres – roughly 1.5 m more than in the building in the Weissenhofsiedlung – and the option of sanitary modules at the core offer room for play, which Mies was unable to explore for technical reasons. The loggias across the full width of the apartment and overlooking the interior of the block also far surpass the standard established by Mies.
Despite the advantages offered by flexible systems, it is difficult to interest investors, buyers and renters for projects of this kind – all the more so, because adaptation to user requirements can only be realized subsequent to initial occupation with a considerable effort that is not commensurate with the standard of a simple apartment dwelling.
A successful project in Berne applied flexibility to the third dimension (ill. 3.8). Apartments, offices, workshops and studios were to be created in accordance with the guidelines established through an investor competition for developing a former industrial site on the Lorrainestrasse. The ground floor, with a room height of 3.5 metres, is designated as a working zone in the new 5-storey building. In addition to apartments, located on the main stairwell, an exterior corridor provides access to maisonette units on the second floor, which feature generous roof patios. The external corridor also provides access to studio apartments, some of which are linked to the working zone on the ground floor. Different living situations and unit sizes are provided thanks to the variable options for linking the floors internally. Load-bearing crosswalls with a centre-to-centre distance of 7.2 metres provide the internal divisions. The only fixed elements in the plan were the position of the stairwell and the service shafts. The tenants were otherwise free to divide the spaces between the apartment walls according to their own wishes and to take influence on the rental costs by choosing different finishing standards. Other forms of flexibility in apartments are designed with the aim of providing spontaneous adaptability by simple,

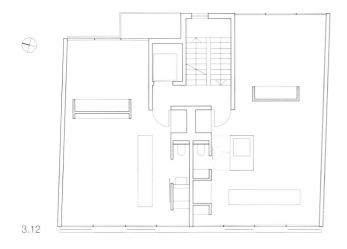

3.12

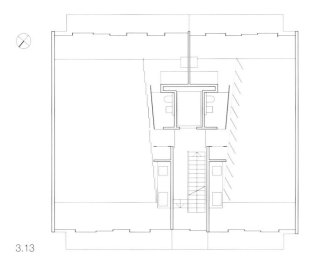

3.13

constructional means. The Viennese architect Herbert Wimmer gives the following reasons for his flexible concepts: "(The concept) must be designed to respond to change quickly and inexpensively. (…) On the one hand, the internal logic of the floor plan must be devised to provide maximum flexibility aside from the essential (and minimized) fixed points; conversely, the technology that enables the flexibility must function without delay."[24] In a small residential building in the Grieshofgasse in Vienna, Wimmer has translated these demands into a floor plan with two, roughly 16.5-m²-large rooms on each side of the building, which can be linked by opening a three-sectioned sliding element (ill. 3.9). Additional 1.6-m-wide sliding doors can also be opened in the transverse direction. One room is designated as a live-in kitchen; the other three are usage neutral.

In another residential building in the Donaufelder Strasse, realized a short time later, Wimmer divided the width of the apartments into three, barely 3-m-wide areas (ill. 3.10). This concept has the advantage that the opening or closing of sliding elements offers a far greater number of combination options and sizes. At the same time, the limitations of this type of flexibility for family living are quickly evident. The absence of conventional hallways and the division of individual spaces by means of mobile walls result in acoustic limitations and greatly diminished possibilities for furniture placement. To Wimmer, the equality of the spaces is an "expression of the equality between all inhabitants, that is, parents and children, man and wife. (…) There is no room here for an expression of power structures."[25] Lucius Burkhardt questions whether this attitude can persist in the face of reality: "A family is not a harmonious configuration; even the happy family operates on the basis of an armistice, which must be maintained in the face of the challenging conditions of rapidly growing opponents, and the resulting shift in the balance of power. Its peace depends on the status quo and this includes the concrete presence of walls. Maintaining this armistice also requires continuity in the interior furnishing of the apartment. Regardless of how mobile a wall may be."[26] Flexible floor plans are more suitable for one- and two-person households than for those with three or more members. Thus Patricia Zacek employs sliding elements in the Siccardsburggasse in Vienna (ill. 3.11) with noticeable restraint. In the south-facing two-room apartments the orientation of the kitchen core toward one side and the door to the sanitary module toward the other side defines the two rooms as living or bedroom zone respectively. If needed, the two principal rooms in the apartment can be combined across the front third of the unit. This spatial overlap relieves the functional definition of the floor plan. In the larger family units, housed in the east-west wing of the ensemble, the architect decided to forego room-connecting sliding doors altogether. Like the smaller units, the bedrooms on the east side are divided from the living and dining area, which opens onto

3.9   Residential building in the Grieshofgasse in Vienna, Herbert Wimmer, 1996, standard floor plan, scale 1:200
3.10 Residential building on Donaufelder Strasse in Vienna, Herbert Wimmer, 1998, standard floor plan, scale 1:200
3.11 Residential building in the Siccardsburggasse in Vienna, Patricia Zacek, 2003, standard floor plan, scale 1:500
3.12 Residential and commercial building on Joachimstrasse in Berlin, Abcarius + Burns, 2001, floor plan for 4th floor, scale 1:200
3.13 Residential building on Choriner Strasse in Berlin, Wolfram Popp, 1998, floor plan option, scale 1:250

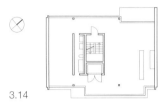

3.14

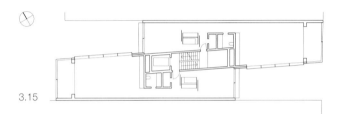

3.15

3.16

a wide loggia overlooking the block interior, by a central access and supply corridor. Bedrooms and bathroom are accessed via a small secondary corridor. In combination with the kitchen, which is open toward the transverse axis of the floor plan, the result is a circular internal path.

For some time now, the loft has evolved from insider tip to effective marketing instrument for distinguished living environments. Peter Faller writes: "The loft as an open living space without internal divisions is the most logical alternative to the floor plan divided according to function; obviously, it is especially compatible with the attitudes and lifestyle of a young generation."[27] Originating as a living space on a converted factory floor, architecture with a loft rating is now often employed to market new buildings, frequently with luxurious completion options. In the building on Joachmistrasse in Berlin, various floor plans are arranged around a stairwell core and installation shaft on 120-m²-large floor levels (ill. 3.12). The area is divided not by walls but by cubes set freely into the space. They contain sanitary modules and built-in cupboards. Concrete ceilings, 26 cm thick and spanning a width of 7 metres, provide space for a wide variety of user requirements. While the large apartment on the second floor is still divided in a fairly conventional manner into zones for day and night by the bathroom and kitchen core, the two smaller units on the fourth floor are far more open in plan. In the north-facing apartment, the door to the shower is set into the outside wall; in the south-facing apartment the shower doors can be slid open to combine with the WC on the opposite side into a three-piece bathroom. Unconventional solutions of this kind are often found in buildings with central stairwell cores. Within the clear dimensions, the open spaces quickly assume their "hard" boundaries in striking contrast to the overall openness.

The access core aside, the internal walls of the estrade house[28] in Berlin can be dissolved completely (ill. 3.13, see also page 154). The floor plans, described by the architect Wolfram Popp as plans for "single-room apartments," can be changed constantly with the help of louvered dividing walls and a range of built-in features chosen by the user, for example, rotating room dividers, movable cabinets and transparent walls. Wooden platforms, 180 cm wide, transition into balconies across the entire width of the facade. Popp explained the point of departure for his concept as follows: "My approach was to create the best possible options for the user's potential needs within the given conditions."[29] After the move-in date for the first, completed building phase, he conceded: "Only one party chose to install a transparent room divider, which separates the front from the back and can be slid wide open, not like a wall but more like a screen. Most of the occupants are singles or couples and not, as I had thought at first, families as well."[30]

For many years, the most elaborate form of access with only one apartment per floor did not play a role in Central European apartment dwellings. Although highly uneconomical, some residential buildings are currently being realized as single-access structures, for example, the building in the Colmarer Strasse in Basel (ill. 3.14). The 165 m² floor area in the apartments, also described as lofts, is divided by the massive stairwell with elevator and the adjacent bathroom. An additional installation shaft for the kitchen increases the options for variation. Doors pushed outward from the core close off a private space when needed. In this case, the

3.17

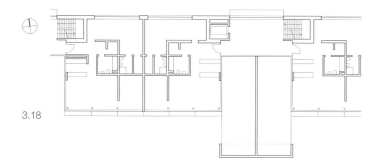

3.18

elevator leads directly into the apartment, independent of the stairs. The purchase price of roughly SwF 700 000 per apartment (ca. € 460,000) is proof of how much features of this kind are appreciated by a certain clientele.

A noticeable feature in some of the aforementioned examples is the lack of closed facade elements. The idea of a "housing shelf" open to the outside seems to be closely associated with the idea of flexibility. It is a manifestation of the need for as little definition as possible: "Because more and more people are working freelance and from home, people opting for these lifestyles require a living environment that is compatible with every step in life. (…) In contrast to the deification of the home as an emotionally charged space that offers 'privacy,' 'optionism' is obviously intended to reconcile the individual with his outside world, with the result, however, of obscuring the real discrepancy between the two."[31]

The "reconciliation" can be achieved in a variety of ways. While the inhabitants of the south-facing two-room apartments in the Siccardsburggasse in Vienna regulate the contact with the streetscape by means of canvas sun shades, the estrade house in Berlin features nearly transparent stainless steel mesh balustrades on the projecting balcony zone as a filter between interior and exterior. Residents in the Grieshofgasse can not only adjust the degree of openness to the outside with the movable screen elements; if they seize the opportunity of embellishing these screens with individual designs they are also following in the footsteps of Hundertwasser – in the spirit of the "Mould Manifesto against Rationalism."[32] A small compensation for the lack of private outdoor space in this project. The building stands in the street like a housing shelf, whose compartments are filled according to the wishes of its inhabitants. The architects Walter Nägeli and Sascha Zander inserted a 7-storey building with deep recesses on both sides into a barely 11-m-wide building gap in Berlin (ills. 3.15, 3.16). Each storey accommodates two staggered apartments, 25 m deep and a maximum of 5.7 m wide. The living/dining area with kitchen faces toward the open corner area, while a sleeping area is lit from one side through the recessed section in the niche. As with other so-called loft concepts, the facade is fully glazed. Floor-to-ceiling sliding doors open onto a small balcony in the recess. The complete transparency is only relieved by an area that is raised by one step and set front of the living room. This zone, called "Mirame," is approximately 2.5 m deep and is intended to serve the inhabitants as a display window. Whether the privacy provided behind this extroverted area is sufficient depends to a great degree on the individual character of the occupants and the floor on which they live. The higher, the more protection the occupants receive from the floor slab against looks from curious passers-by. This project clearly demonstrates that fully transparent facades in densely built-up areas fail to provide a sufficient degree of privacy. One can hardly imagine a building

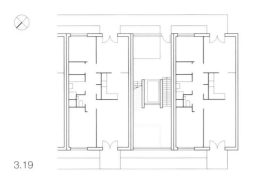

3.19

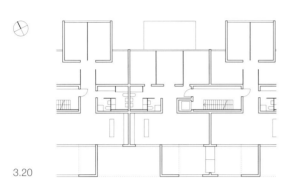

3.20

3.21

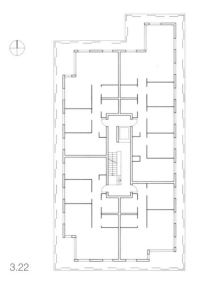

3.22

with a similarly transparent facade "staring back" from the opposite side of the street. Such glass cubes are more likely to remain exclusive one-of-a-kind objects for a clientele that is willing to accept a minimum of privacy for the certainty of differentiating themselves from the conventional masses. The sociologist Ulrich Beck comments: "However, what is individualization to one person is often the limit of individualization to another."[33]

The Private Exterior Space

The home and the private exterior space is one of the few areas where the influences of the outside world can still be measured out at one's own discretion. In apartment buildings, private exterior spaces – often placed at the transition from public to private space – are particularly exposed. In projects with lower glazing ratios in the facade, additional spaces for personal use are frequently developed out of the private exterior space, which only serves to underscore the introverted character of the former.
The plastic building slabs of the staff residence on the Stuttgart Burgholzhof have nothing in common with contemporary facade designs dominated by glazed structural elements (ill. 3.17). The volumes, cut deep into the structure, convey an image of shelter. Fibre-cement panels, coated in a transparent glaze of brilliant colours, mark the access elements and relieve the grey varnish on the facades and the box windows, the outer layer of which consists of single-glazed sliding elements that are flush with the facade. On the wall surface, carefully faced with vertical battening, light is redirected into the depth of the apartment. The tall balcony balustrade frames the view from the inside and transforms the outdoor seating area into an extension of the interior space. With even deeper recesses, a building by Martin Spühler in Zurich-Oerlikon (ill. 3.18, see also p. 142) is distantly related to Le Corbusier's *"Immeubles Villas"* from 1922. Large openings in the south row relieve the narrow, slightly over 20-m-deep interior courtyard of the housing block. The 90-m-long facade is divided into three roughly 7.5-m-deep and 10-m-wide loggia zones. Access to the two apartments per floor is provided via a stair- and elevator core to the rear. The private living area is complemented by two additional zones in this project: with an area of more than 30 m², the semi-public access area in front of the apartment door can function as a balcony alternative in cold weather and a play area for children, and the loggia with central division is an adequate private exterior space, also 30 m² in size. The large living, dining and cooking area is oriented toward this loggia. While Le Corbusier envisioned loggias extended across two storeys, Martin Spühler seeks to improve the lighting of his single-storey areas by means of a large skylight above the landing in front of the apartment door. The conflict that arises in this area between the desire for privacy and maximum transparency across the building

3.19   Block edge development Stadstuinen in Rotterdam, KCAP, 2002, standard floor plan, scale 1:500
3.20   Residential building on Paul-Clairmont-Strasse in Zurich-Wiedikon, Jakob Steib and Patrick Gmür, completion scheduled for 2005, standard floor plan, scale 1:500
3.21   Residential building on Paltramplatz in Vienna, Delugan Meissl, 2002, floor plan for 6th floor, scale 1:500
3.22, 3.23 "Achslengut" housing complex in St Gallen, Baumschlager Eberle, 2002, standard floor plan, scale 1:500, exterior view

depth with good lighting for the inner core is not easily solved. Like the project in Zurich, the senior's apartments in the Stadstuined district of Rotterdam also feature two different exterior spaces in addition to the actual living area (ill. 3. 19, see also p. 160). A roughly 2-m-deep zone with high ceilings and entrance landings lies behind the glazed exterior corridor on the east side. These areas in front of the apartment doors, approximately 5 m² in size, can thus be utilized as weather-protected contact zones. The apartment door, with a double window, leads into a reception area, which can also be used as a dining area. This connects through the centrally located kitchen to the actual living room or to a small corridor, which provides access to the sanitary modules and one room overlooking the glazed exterior corridor. Glazed oriels suspended in front of the clinker-faced facade on the north-west side alternate in use from floor to floor as winter gardens and balconies. Here, the view is not blocked by closed balustrades. How successful these spaces are despite the high degree of transparency is evident in the amount of furnishings in the exterior spaces of some units. Areas are thus provided on both sides of the apartment for the communication needs of residents with limited mobility. They benefit from a safe sheltered area behind the double windows. In addition to their principal function, balconies are also frequently employed as design means to relieve the monotony of the facade. Otto Steidle, for example, added projecting balconies to the apartment tower in Munich's Theresienhöhe district. However, the seemingly random arrangement of the balconies suggests that they are employed to animate the facade rather than provide functional outdoor spaces for the individual apartments. Their utility is strongly compromised

3.23

by the lack of visual screening from adjacent balconies and the limited shading.

Exterior spaces can make a greater contribution to the private sphere when the boundaries are more enclosed. It is important, however, to ensure that they do not have an adverse effect on the lighting of the interior living space. A south-facing, 7-storey staggered housing row is currently being erected on Paul-Clairmont-Strasse in Zurich (ill. 3.20). The core structure is complemented on both sides by offset additions. On the north side, every second apartment features an element with two rooms in front of the house edge. Cubes, open on the top, are attached as outdoor spaces in front of the living areas on the opposite side. The set backs of these patios from floor to floor in combination with the centred storage boxes in front of each unit create a high-quality, spatially differentiated exterior space with an area considerably greater than 20 m². The walls surrounding this outdoor space offer excellent visual protection. Despite a patio depth of nearly 4 metres, the 2-storey open space provides good lighting for the living areas behind it. The space beneath the single-storey area acts as a shady retreat, reminiscent of modern housing in warmer climate zones. The project is an impressive illustration of the growing importance of exterior space. In the facade of the Rubik house by Delugan and Meissl on Vienna's Paltramplatz, only the loggias are glazed from floor to ceiling with openable elements from the balustrade up (ill. 3.21). They are the principal feature in the facade design; light to the living rooms, on the other hand, is provided through smaller windows of varying sizes and positions. They penetrate the anthracite-tinted building skin and even project slightly beyond the outside edge. Mediating between interior

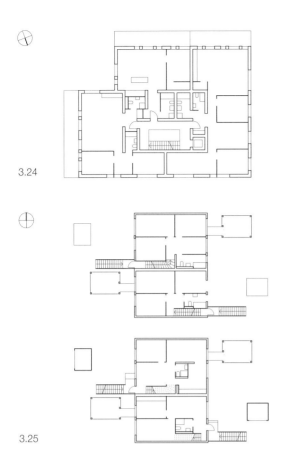

3.24

3.25

3.26

and exterior, these glass cubes are the point where private apartment and public space come into contact. The inhabitants can withdraw into the interior at any time. The apartments are arranged in groups of three around a central stairwell. Although the floor plans are less striking than the facade concept, they nevertheless provide favourable conditions for appropriation by the occupants because they are somewhat screened from the curious gaze of passers-by. The architects Baumschlager and Eberle have perfected the solitary building type over the past ten years in a series of projects. Increasing in size and density over time, this type has reached its preliminary high point in the Lohbach development in Innsbruck. The Achslengut housing complex in St. Gallen, built two years later, was created according to the same principle (ills. 3.22, 3.23): the floor plan progresses in layers, like an onion, from the inside out. An inner core provides access to four apartments per floor. The ancillary rooms are arranged around this core, accommodating the services required for the actual living space oriented toward the outside. The exterior walls are surrounded by a perimeter balcony zone, marked on the outside by autonomous facade elements. In their previous developments, the architects frequently designed the principal building fabric and the envelope as rectangles with different dimensions, creating an interstitial space wrapped around the building. In St. Gallen, on the other hand, the rooms are recessed at the corners. The balcony zones are transformed into areas for specific individual uses that are at some distance from each other – an advantageous arrangement with regard to acoustics. The selection of materials, too, has changed over time. Whereas the copper folding shutters in the external skin can be opened and closed individually in the Lohbach development, the St. Gallen complex offers the possibility of sliding the translucent glass elements into various positions. But the fundamental character of the double layer remains. The significance of the actual house wall plays second fiddle to the external skin. The sheltered open space on each level, resulting from these arrangements, creates favourable conditions for making it one's own without exposing private objects in a distracting or unattractive manner.

The 5-storey buildings on Hegianwandweg (ill. 3.24, see also p. 46) were also realized in the context of the program launched in Zurich under the title "10 000 new apartments in 10 years." The detached blocks are attached to a plinth structure accommodating the shared underground garage. Despite the implications with regard to fire protection and projected additional costs of 1.5 per cent by comparison to a massive construction method, the choice was to erect a multi-storey timber structure – a complete departure from the standard practice in Switzerland. The concrete access core, which also contains the sanitary modules of the units, is surrounded by a timber construction that provides a great deal of flexibility for the internal divisions. The spatial program is complemented by a projecting balcony zone, which comprises the third layer. Access to the units, ranging in size from 64 to 139 m², with rooms that are no less than 13.5 m², is provided via private entrance corridors. The living- and dining areas, spacious at over 28 m², are oriented to at least to two or three sides. Some of the apartments are even equipped with two balconies facing in different directions and with a total exterior living area of more than 60 m². As in the estrade house in Berlin, the generous balcony areas are surrounded by in semi-transparent balustrades. These 2-m-wide and in some cases over 15-m-long "sun rooms" are also fitted with external blinds. When pulled down to the balustrade, they create a private, shaded external space with the characteristics of an internal gallery. Seen from the outside, the aspect with closed balcony shutters results in a somewhat jarring reversal of what one would expect to see: the closed balustrades and the horizontal, transparent bands of windows of modern purpose architecture. The balcony zones with the deep, projecting ceilings and the blinds are small, fronting volumes that obscure the true dimensions of the blocks, thereby softening the leap in scale by comparison to the surrounding built environment. In contrast to the balcony zones, the principal fabrics appear rather closed, even though some of the openings cut into them are also very generous in size. The question whether an alternative to the ventilated stucco facade, which meets the fire-protection regulations, would have been more compatible with the timber construction remains unanswered.[34]

Frank Zieraus' residential towers with balconies stand as fully detached structures in front of the 4-storey housing rows in another Zurich district (ill. 3.25). On the Burriweg, pairs of maisonettes stacked one above the other, share a 10-m-high timber structure. The loggias, set off from the principal volume by roughly 2 metres, are clad in fine battens with openings at window height in three directions to offer an unobstructed view of the outside. The entrances to the apartments are located on the opposite side. The upper unit is reached via a single flight of stairs, clad in wooden slats and also set off from the principal volume. The entrance to the lower unit is located at garden level beneath the stair landing. Single-storey storage sheds are the third element set off from the principal volume on the same side, in this case with the greatest distance to the building. The position of the three additional wooden structures alternates from side to side as does the access point from unit to unit. The block with access from the east differs from its 7.5-m-wide counterpart, accessed from the west, only in that it is slightly less wide at roughly 6.4 metres. The result is a rich variation in volumes, acting as visual screens and determining the sightlines. Far surpassing the possibilities of conventional divisions, small walls and plantings, the spaces between the rows are divided in a multitude of ways and are readily transformed into private outdoor spaces.

With the increased estimation for private outdoor space, terraced housing is experiencing a renaissance. The most common type follows the contour of a steep slope. The resulting set backs on each floor create large, usually south-facing outdoor spaces. In the Netherlands and in Belgium, there has been a return in recent years to building terraced housing on level ground. The degree of privacy on the balconies is regulated by 'packaging' the latter in a more or less intensive fashion. In the terraced house, conversely, the decisive factor is the distance between adjacent outdoor spaces. While the irregular arrangement of balconies on the facade tends to require additional effort in terms of screening, the irregular arrangement of terraces can even enhance

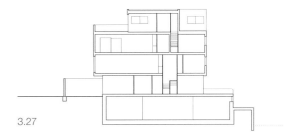

3.27

3.28

3.24   Residential building on Hegianwandweg in Zurich,
         EM2N Mathias Müller and Daniel Niggli, 2003,
         standard floor plan, scale 1:500
3.25   Burriweg housing rows in Zurich, Frank Zierau, 2002,
         floor plans for ground floor and 2nd floor, scale 1:500
3.26 to 3.28 The Hollainhof in Gent, Neutelings Riedijk, 1998,
         eastern housing row, floor plans for 3rd and 4th floor, section,
         scale 1:500, exterior view

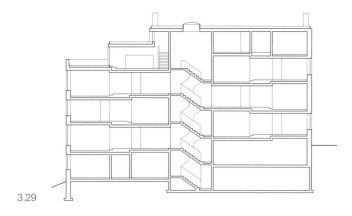

3.29

the privacy offered by these outdoor spaces. With its cubic appearance, the Hollainhof in Gent has little in common with a classic terraced house (ills. 3.26–3.28). Based on a rigorous 4-m-grid, two 4-storey housing rows overlook a green zone in the middle. The western row with a plinth storey lies parallel to the street; the eastern row borders on a canal. On this side, single-axis maisonette units, over 15 metres in depth, have small garden courtyards on both sides. The private entrances to the flats and maisonettes on the second and third floor are located on open landings. These units benefit from the deep set backs and recesses in the building volume, with room-sized private outdoor spaces on both sides, which are close to nature and at the same time sheltered from the elements and prying eyes.

Interior Space

The spatial qualities in high-density housing frequently mirror the deficiencies in plan and elevation. Even most of the new single-family house developments repeat the same monotonous pattern of stacking a bedroom floor on top of a living floor, for cost efficiency and also due to a lack in imagination. The three-dimensional potentials are often unrealized. Recently, however, there are more and more counter proposals for liberating the apartment from its narrow confines between floor slabs with the help of effective spatial solutions. Emulating the idea of Loos' spatial plan – differentiated room heights corresponding to function – several recent projects feature staggered ceiling heights or, more precisely, raised ceilings. Building upon the spatial concept of the "Brenner-block" in Frankfurt (1929), the architect Jakob Steib has differentiated the room heights in the single-storey apartments in the Kurfürst house in Zurich according to function (ill. 3.29). The 3-m-high living areas alternate with 2.4-m-high bedroom and auxiliary areas. Using two steps at floor level and a ceiling raised by the same measure, Steib expands the spatial boundaries of the units in the building for nine families in an elegant fashion. The transition between high-ceilinged living room and the lower areas is located at the same position in the floor plans of the units above and below to accommodate the different room heights without additional building volume. The differences in ceiling height are compensated in the load-bearing walls in the room axes. This is an advantage by comparison to Anton Brenner's historic construction, where the dividing wall of each unit runs across the centre of the ceiling of the apartment below. Conceived as a building with two apartments per floor, the result is a dramatic, three-dimensional interaction enhanced by the slight deviations in plan and elevation.

Developed from split-level concepts for the Berlin Interbau fair in 1957, the City-Lofts on the Wienerberg are especially promising from a spatial perspective (ill. 3.30). Eight main floors on the north side are allocated to six taller floors on the south side in a building with two commercial floors at ground level. Internal stairs in the centre of the building bridge the resulting differences in height. The 3.3-m-high space on the south side has a positive impact on the lighting of the 16-m-deep floor plans. The smaller rooms on the north side, by contrast, barely reach a height of 2.3 metres. Apartments with a centre-to-centre distance of roughly 4.5 metres alternate with the 6.5-m-wide types. Individual allocation of the zones with differing room heights means that none of the front-to-back apartments are identical. The entrances are

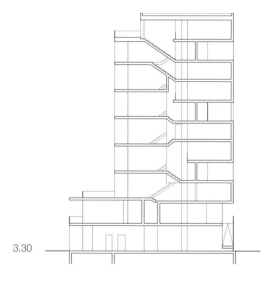

3.30

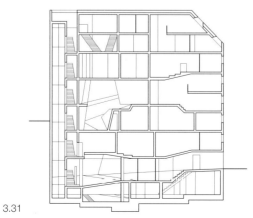

3.31

3.32

similarly distinct due to a meandering access zone across the length of the building. The goal of strongly differentiated apartments is thus achieved without running the risk of creating a confusing maze of access corridors.

Two Viennese projects, which are remarkable in many ways, also possess spatial characteristics that go far beyond the conventional standard of an apartment. In the building, which has been dubbed the "Sargfabrik" or "coffin factory," many units feature a 2-storey living room with loft and galleries. In the successor, the so-called "Miss Sargfabrik," additional amenities were relocated from the usual isolation in dark basement floors to the upper levels (ills. 3.31, 3.32). The laundry room, for example, is located on the fifth floor, linked via a glass wall with the home library and the access area into a stunning, semi-public space with some uneven planes. This unusual combination, together with its elevated position, makes a considerable contribution to improving the communication within the building. The additional shared facilities such as kindergarten, pool, event auditorium and Café became financially feasible by opening them to the community. This implicit obligation to include outsiders acts as a strong unifying trigger for the entire neighbourhood.

The so-called "Kraftwerk 1" complex in Zurich is equally ambitious in terms of the spatial and social program (ill. 3.33). Inspired by the social ideas of the 1980s, a group of fifty people formed a co-operative in the mid-90s with the goal of creating a vital neighbourhood on an industrial wasteland. To this end, they developed a concept for 106 apartments and over 3300 m^2 of commercial space distributed across four buildings complemented by, among other things, offices, a restaurant, stores and a kindergarten. The 8-storey main building faces east-west. The bottom half of the building is divided into four bedroom levels on the east side allocated to three floors designated as living zones on the west side. This results in 20-m-deep plans with split-level units of varying sizes. Some of the 2- to 13-room apartments stretch across three floors and occupy a varying number of centre-to-centre axes, each 4 metres wide. The largest suite boasts over 350 m^2 in living area and can accommodate a large household or co-operative. Light falls through the 3.2-m-high common rooms deep into the space all the way to the internal split-level stairs. At a minimum size of 14 m^2, the individual rooms are ideally suited as private withdrawing areas. But the units also offer much larger rooms of 20 m^2 and more. Altogether, the district offers a lively combination of more than 100 workplaces and housing for 300 people. Many of the original ideas, such as car-sharing, photovoltaics, district heating and heat recovery, were successfully realized. To finance the co-op facilities, however, the tenants must contribute SwF 15000 (ca. 10000 €) per 35 m^2 of living area.[35] Nevertheless, there is great demand for the apartments in this complex. This may be seen as confirmation of the need for forward-thinking social projects, albeit only for a small niche market

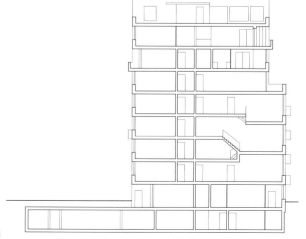

3.33

3.29 Residential building Kurfürst in Zurich, Jakob Steib, 2000, section, scale 1:500
3.30 City-Lofts on the Wienerberg in Vienna, Delugan Meissl, 2004, section, scale 1:500
3.31, 3.32 "Miss Sargfabrik" residential building in Vienna, BKK 3, 2000, section, scale 1:500, view into laundry room
3.33 "Kraftwerk 1" housing complex in Zurich, Stücheli Architekten, 2001, section, scale 1:500

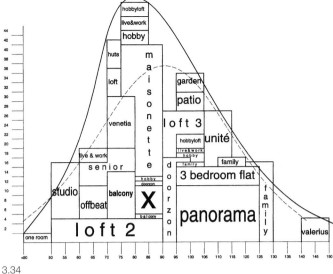

3.34

3.35

because of the intensive and lengthy preparation phase that is required. Hence concepts such as "Kraftwerk 1" remain the exception.

The Simulated Apartment

New methods are increasingly simulating more complex planning processes. The Dutch team of architects MVRDV, for example, employ a computer program, the so-called "functionmixer" to play with parameters such as density, site conditions and use on a virtual plane, before selecting the optimal variation from a series of possibilities, which is then explored in detail. In addition to regional planning tasks, tools of this kind can also contribute solutions for urban planning and architectural problems. Their use can even change housing construction itself. Preliminary studies for the Amsterdam project "Silodamm" were used to search for an ideal mix and distribution of uses. The result is a hybrid building with 157 apartments, offices, commercial spaces and public facilities. Groups of four to eight typologically identical apartments are combined into miniature neighbourhoods with distinctive facade features that distinguish them clearly from the other apartment groupings in the 10-storey building. Nathalie de Vries speaks of a "museum of types," with which the architects MVRDV have responded to the changed situation: "The demand for greater variety and unusual housing solutions is getting out of hand. The ideal house has seen its day; there are thousands of ideal houses."[36] Every conceivable type of apartment is accommodated and stacked into the 20-m-deep and 10-storey-high structure: access via interior or exterior corridors, flats and maisonettes, condominiums and rental units. Twenty different apartment types are reflected in an equal number of facade variations on the outside. Surrounded by water on three sides, the structure has the appearance of a self-sufficient "steamship" about to set sail. Whether the heterogeneity of the apartment groups in this "patchwork unité" is perceived as a mark of quality remains to be seen.

Unique, functionally customized architecture recedes into the background when variable building systems, which make it possible to optimize a wide variety of individual solutions, are employed. Frank-Bertolt Raith and Rob van Gool, who undertook a detailed study of the housing industry in the Netherlands over the past decade, predict that single-family homes will be produced in series and that this trend will be accompanied by a new understanding of the role of architecture, "which no longer works towards 'elevating' the standard with an educational and artistic intent, but takes the wishes of the client seriously – regardless of whether they agree with one's own ideas or not."[37]

Interactive Internet platforms already provide potential buyers with the option of participating in the planning of single-family homes. On the American site "etekt.com" anyone can present ideas, which are then optimized in several interactive stages in collaboration with partners who are willing to execute the design. This sounds appealing to all sides: users get perfectly customized products, the building industry can operate efficiently with standardized building components, and architects have found a new forum for their ideas.

The question arises how much time will pass before every layperson can compose his or her own dream house with the help of ever more perfect simulation models and then purchase it as a manufactured turnkey product. It would seem that the new options for participation are widening the gap between the little house – detached or semi-detached – as an ideal housing model and high-density housing solutions. Beck's thesis on the limitations of individualization – which states that increased density also increases the significance of binding rules – is as valid as ever.

There is still time before simulation programs like the "functionmixer," which are used to determine density, mixed use and spatial quality, are diminished to serving only the economic interests. This time could be utilized, for example, to further develop Mies van der Rohe's idea of a flexible structure, especially since few end users of apartments enjoy the same freedom today as was granted to his "design architects" for the interiors of the Weissenhof. The realization of convincing housing concepts where occupants are granted free expression even on the facade is still a long way off, although interesting proposals are repeatedly made in this direction.

Cities and regions will grow even more competitive in view of stagnating or even decreasing population figures. They will try to attract highly educated, young and affluent inhabitants. Against this background we can look forward to the realization of more innovative ideas. As in the examples above, the developments will aim for a high degree of adaptability, good opportunities for withdrawing into a private sphere and large living areas. While new construction continues to play only a secondary role in the housing sector by comparison to the large inventory of existing housing, innovative and qualitative buildings can act as positive force, helping to recast the image of the ideal home among broad sectors in the population from detached villa toward high-density forms of housing.

Notes:

1 Walter Benjamin, Denkbilder (1932), Gesammelte Schriften IV, Frankfurt am Main, vol. 1, p. 404

2 Internationale Kongresse für Neues Bauen, Zurich (ed.), Die Wohnung für das Existenzminimum, (Frankfurt am Main, 1930); see also: Gerd Kuhn, Wohnkultur und kommunale Wohnungspolitik in Frankfurt am Main von 1880–1930. (Bonn, 1998)

3 Ludwig Mies van der Rohe, Bau und Wohnung, p. 77; cited in: Karin Kirsch, The Weissenhofsiedlung: Experimental Housing Built for the Deutscher Werkbund, Stuttgart, 1927, transl. David Britt, (New York: Rizzoli, 1989), p. 47

4 Karin Kirsch, op. cit., pp. 59

5 The so-called Neubühl Group of the Swiss Werkbund was led by Max Ernst Haefeli and included the following members: Ernst F. Burckhardt, Karl Egender, Alfred Gradmann, Hans Hofmann, Wilhelm Kienzle, Werner M. Moser, Hans Weisse, R.S. Rütschi, Rudolf Steiger, Franz Scheibler, Paul Artaria and Hans Schmid. See Karin Kirsch, op. cit., p. 85.

6 Planned by the representatives of professional women after designs by H. Zimmermann, R. and M. Stotz and W. Schneider in House 1, apartment 1, ground floor, right. See Karin Kirsch, op. cit., p. 69.

7 Gert Kähler, "Kollektive Struktur, individuelle Interpretation" in: arch + 100/101, p. 43.

8 Federal Statistical Office, statistical yearbook 2003, p. 243; 10.6 Approved and completed apartments

9 Federal Statistical Office, Living and Working in Germany, results of the sample census 2002, Wiesbaden 2003

10 Annette Spellerberg, Lebensstile und Wohnprofile: Trends, in: Krüger, Kirsten / Brech, Joachim, Wohnwandel. (Darmstadt, 2001), pp. 276 See also: Andritzky, Michael, Balance zwischen Heim und Welt, in: Ingeborg Flagge (ed.): Geschichte des Wohnens, (Stuttgart, 1999), vol. V, pp. 672

11 Annette Spellerberg, op. cit., p. 282

12 Federal Statistical Office, statistical yearbook 2003; 10.11 Condominium and rental apartments in April 1998 according to living area and construction year, p. 248; see also: Harlander, Tilman (ed.), Villa und Eigenheim, Suburbaner Städtebau in Deutschland, (Ludwigsburg, Stuttgart, Munich, 2001)

13 Jörg Scheufele, "Planen Architekten am Kunden vorbei?" in: Baumeister 7/2003, p. 59.

14 Switzerland: apartments in single- and semi-detached houses/home ownership rates 37% / 31% (1990), Germany 46% / 41% (1998), the Netherlands 71% / 52% (1999), Spain 40% / 81% (1999); in: Wüstenrot Stiftung (ed.), Wohneigentum in Europa, (Ludwigsburg, 2002)

15 Argast, Frank / Kurz, Daniel, 10 000 Wohnungen und 100 neue Ideen. In: Stand der Dinge, Neustes Wohnen in Zürich, exhibition catalogue, (Zurich, 2002)

16 Bern: Stadtentwicklungskonzept Bern, Fortschreibung Wohnen (STEK 95). See: Stand der Dinge, Wohnen in Bern, exhibition catalogue, (Zurich, 2003). Basel: In the context of the "Logis Bâle" program, a plan has been launched to create 5000 family-friendly and high-quality apartments over the next ten years; see also: www.Basel.ch

17 Tränkle, Margret, Neue Wohnungshorizonte. In: Ingeborg Flagge, op. cit., p. 764

18 Matthias Horx, Zwischen Konvention und Innovation – Wandel des Wohnens. In: Wüstenrot Stiftung (ed.), Wohnbauen in Deutschland, (Stuttgart, 2002), p. 211

19 Karin Zapf. In: Ingeborg Flagge, op. cit., p. 583

20 See, for example, Kassel Rothenberg 1929–31. In: Peter Faller, Der Wohngrundriß. (Stuttgart, Munich, 2002), p. 315

21 Jörg Scheufele, op. cit.

22 Matthias Horx, op. cit.

23 Similar bathroom access solutions are found, among others, in the housing development on the park in Oerlikon by Martin Spühler, in Jakob Steib's Kurfürst house and in the Wehrenbachhalde ensemble by Burkhalter+Sumi

24 Herbert Wimmer, Wohn-Optionen. In: Dworschak, Gunda/ Wenke, Alfred (eds.), Zukunft Wohnen, (Augsburg, 1998), p. 186

25 Herbert Wimmer, op. cit., p. 187

26 Lucius Burckhardt, "Die Kinder fressen ihre Revolution." In: arch+ 100/101, p. 20

27 Peter Faller, Der Wohngrundriß, (Stuttgart, Munich, 2002), p. 67

28 estrade = a slightly raised platform in a room or hall, from the Spanish estrado, part of a room in which a carpet is spread. See: Random House Unabridged Dictionary, 2nd edition, New York, 1987, p. 664

29 Wolfram Popp in conversation with Max Glauner on the occasion of the Architekturforum Linz, 1999, cited from www.popp-planungen.de/html/max.html

30 Wolfram Popp, op. cit.

31 Michael Kasicke reporting on the style/trends study. In: Bauwelt 5/2003, p. 31

32 Friedensreich Hundertwasser, (1928–2000), "Mould Manifesto against rationalism in architecture." (1958) In: Conrads, Ulrich (ed.), Programmes and manifestoes on 20th-century architecture (London: Lund Humphries, 1970), pp. 157

33 Ulrich Beck, "Individualisierung, Globalisierung und Politik." In: arch+ 158, p. 29

34 Swiss fire protection regulations, which are especially restrictive, are currently being adapted to European standards. See: Hochparterre 10/2003, p. 18

35 see: www.kraftwerk1.ch

36 Cited in: Neue Zürcher Zeitung, March 7, 2003

37 Raith, Frank-Bertolt and van Gool, Rob, "Jenseits des Standards." In: arch+ 158, p. 65

3.34, 3.35 "Silodam" housing row in Amsterdam, MVRDV, 2002, diagram of uses and elevation

Table of projects according to materials used

Timber

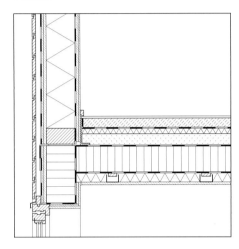

Steel

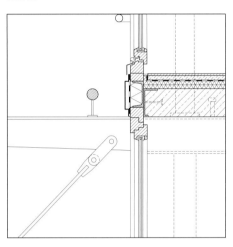

Concrete

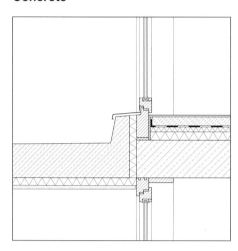

Brickwork and stone

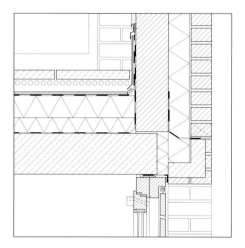

Housing Development in Zurich

Architects: EM2N Architects, Zurich

Site plan   scale 1:4000
Isometric diagram of construction process

Glowing light green fabric sunshades contrasting with the severe rendered walls define the image of the latest cooperative housing development on the outskirts of Zurich. Between schools, multi-storey apartment buildings and a 1950s housing development, five dark grey cubes raised on a concrete pedestal call attention to themselves. They are home to 74 dwellings, two kindergartens, two studios and a community room. Generously planned, glazed entries, pragmatic zones for letter boxes and the parking of prams and pushers, provide the transition from the central asphalt plaza to the stairwells of these four and five storey buildings. Each storey provides three or four corner dwellings, a third of which can claim lighting from three directions. These dwellings, however, can also be individually designed and altered as desired, whether as a multi-room family home or a single-room loft. When one enters these dwellings one may either pass through a long corridor past various rooms to the living room, or directly into a generous one-room apartment. The two-metre deep balconies, which face either south, east or west, can be internalised by the lowering of vertical fabric sun-shades to extend the living areas of the dwellings outwards. They are reached through ceiling height glazed doors.

This housing development was constructed as a test case for multi-storey timber and concrete mixed construction techniques. Five braced concrete cores containing the stairwells, lifts, entries and bathrooms project out of the flat basement carpark roof. Fixed to these cores are the solid horizontally "stacked board" timber slabs which span to the external load bearing timber framed walls. The resultant column-free storeys allow almost total freedom in the planning of the dwellings, whilst also ensuring flexibility for future alterations, in the use of non-load-bearing partition walling. A timber beam extends every 60 cm from the "stacked board" timber slabs providing support for the cantilevered balconies. The balconies and floors are constructionally a single unit with only minimal cold-bridging occuring. Cement-fibre sheeting was clad on both the external and internal faces of the extensively insulated external walls prior to rendering; they were then finished with an internal plasterboard cavity wall subsequent to electrical and plumbing installations. The use of prefabricated timber elements resulted not only in an environmentally friendly product, but also allowed a compacted construction time. This housing development complies with low energy standards through the further application of a few additional measures, such as controlled ventilation and the recycling of "lost" thermal energy.

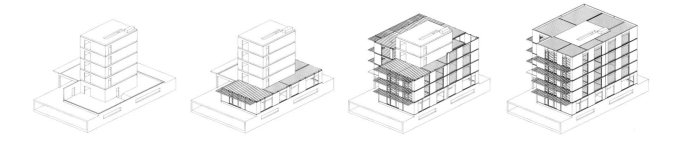

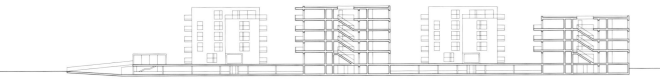

aa

Section • Floor plans   scale 1:1000

A Roof level
B Upper floor
C Ground floor

Listing of dwellings
according to area, in m²:
1 2½-room apartments
2 3½-room apartments
3 4½-room apartments
4 5½-room apartments
5 Studio
6 Hobby room
7 Community room

Project details:
Usage: 74 dwelling units
                        2 kindergartens
                        2 studios
                        1 community room
Units: 14× 2½-room apartments
                        (64–72 m²)
                        23× 3½-room apartments
                        (93 m²)
                        29× 4½-room apartments
                        (105–122 m²)
                        8× 5½-room apartments
                        (137–139 m²)
Internal room height: 2.42–2.50 m
Construction: Reinforced concrete
                        cores with timber
                        construction floors and
                        facades
Unit access: multi-dwelling access
                        units
Total floor area: 14,404 m²
Total site area: 12,896 m²
Construction time: Jan 2002 – Jul 2003

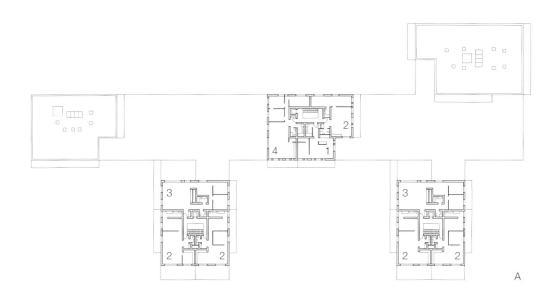

A

B

C

49

Sections   scale 1:20

 1 Roof construction:
    Planting 80 mm
    Drainage membrane 20 mm
    Polymer bituminous sheeting
    Mineral wool with gradient 150–200 mm
    "Stacked board" timber slab 180 mm
    Mineral wool insulation 30 mm
    Plasterboard 2× 12.5 mm
 2 Laminated timber lintel 63 × 360 mm
 3 Wall construction:
    Cement fibre sheeting 11 mm, painted
    Windproof membrane
    Plaster fibreboard 15 mm
    Timber stud 180 mm
    Mineral fibreboard 180 mm
    Plaster fibreboard 15 mm
    Vapour barrier
    Mineral wool insulation 30 mm
    Plasterboard 2× 12.5 mm
 4 Timber window with double glazing
 5 Terrace construction:
    Concrete pavers 400 × 400 × 40 mm
    Gravel 40–80 mm
    Impermeable membrane
    3-ply boarding 27 mm
    Laminated timber beam 100 × 200 mm
    Batten 24 × 48 mm
    Cement fibre sheeting 11 mm, painted
 6 Stainless steel gutter
 7 Floor construction room:
    Oak parquet flooring 10 mm
    Screed 70 mm
    PE membrane
    Sound insulation 30 mm, Membrane
    "Stacked board" timber slab 200 mm
    Mineral wool insulation 30 m
    Plasterboard 2× 12.5 mm
 8 Sealing mortar
 9 Floor construction hall:
    Cast stone tile 20 mm
    Cement screed 60 mm
    PE membrane
    Sound insulation 30 mm
    Reinforced concrete 220mm
10 Balcony construction:
    Douglas fir timber grid 25 × 100 mm
    Aluminium channel 30 × 68 × 3 mm
    Wedge batten 40 mm
    Synthetic matting
    Impermeable membrane
    Reinforced concrete 220 mm
    Batten 24 × 48 mm
    Sheeting 16 mm, Render
11 Vertical awning
12 Floor entrance:
    Asphalt 80 mm
    Polymer bituminous membrane
    Reinforced concrete 350 mm
13 Stainless steel gutter

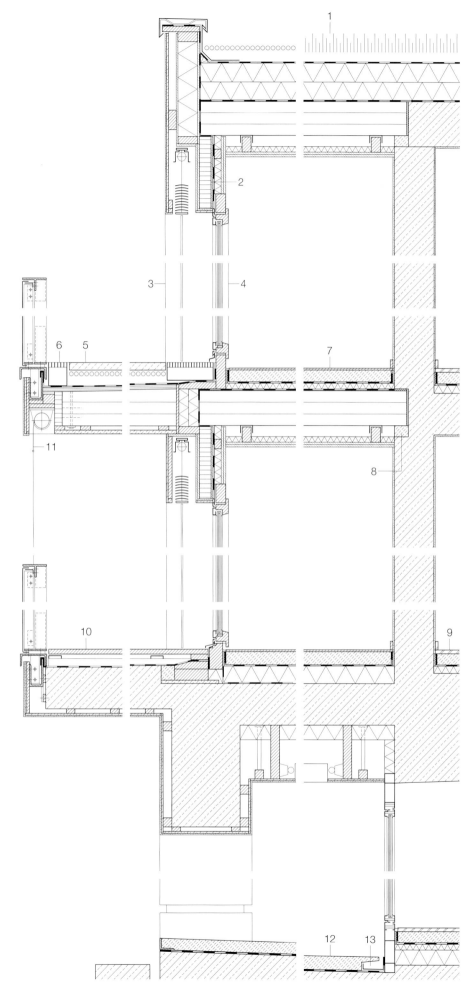

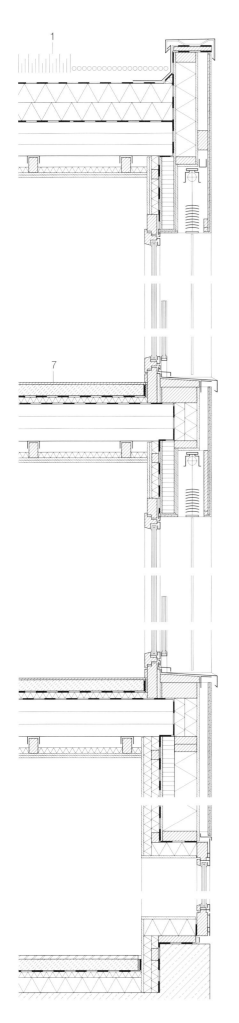

1

7

Housing Block in Merano

Architects: Holzbox Tirol, Innsbruck
in collaboration with Anton Höss, Innsbruck

At the edge of the city centre of Merano, surrounded by residental and light industrial developments, a new housing block was created for young families, couples and singles. In size and function, this four storey building corresponds to the surrounding developments; its formal language and choice of materials, however, are strikingly different in appearance. The dwellings open towards the south-west through spacious loggias supported by cantilevered cross-walling. Sunshading and visual screening is provided by coloured fabric panels.

The lively chequerboard pattern created by these elements reveals the storey-wise reversal of the internal planning of the dwellings. The central core zone of bathrooms and open kitchens divides the dwellings into two living areas, oriented towards north-east and south-west, while still allowing views in both directions. A steel structure with access galleries, stairs and a lift is attached to the block along the north-east elevation, to the road, and the south-east elevation. Flooring and steps are in larch timber and the fine metal mesh screens will, over time, be covered with climbing plants and become green filters.

The clear structural composition of large-scale, prefabricated, solid timber panels achieves great rigidity and strength, simultaneously ensuring ease of assembly and providing thermal storage mass. The architects claim the system can be applied to buildings of ten storeys or more.

A covered communal terrace on the roof is flanked by solar collectors and large planting basins for palm trees, the weight of which is equivalent to two additional storeys, further demonstrating the load-bearing capacity of the system.

Site plan
scale 1:1000
Floor plans
scale 1:250

1 Kitchen
2 Bedroom
3 Living room

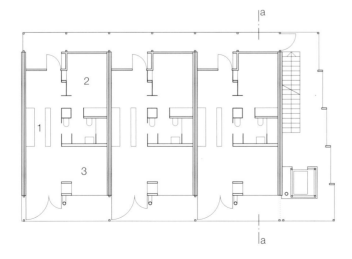

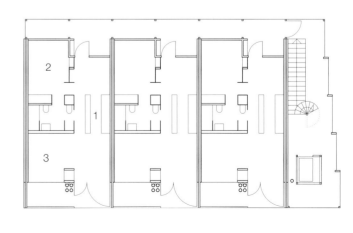

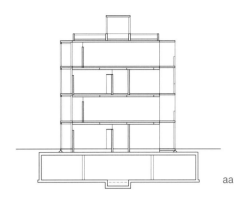

aa

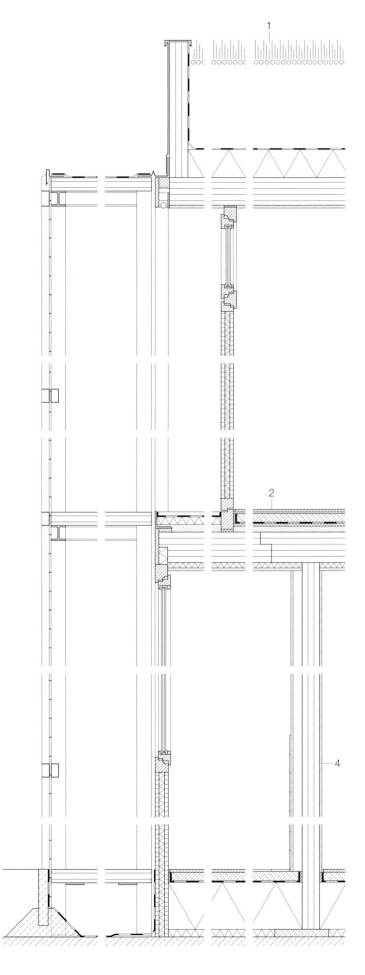

Project details:
Usage: 12 dwelling units
Units: 12× 2½-room apartments (50 m²)
Internal room height: 2.60 m
Construction: Timber panel construction
Unit access: Covered walkway apartments
Total floor area: 781 m²
Total site area: 637 m²
Construction time: Oct 2002 – Dec 2003

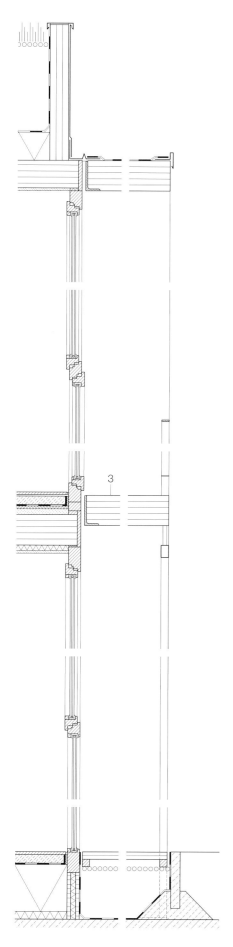

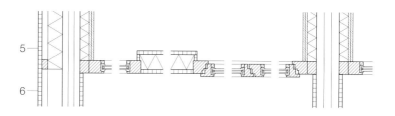

Section   scale 1:400
Vertical section · Horizontal section   scale 1:20

1 500 mm planted layer
   5 mm sealing layer on 150 mm soft fibreboard
   thermal insulation
   146 mm lam. fir-plank element,
   layers glued at right angles to each other
   15 mm plasterboard
2 13 mm parquet, 2 mm separating layer
   45 mm floated screed, separating layer
   15 mm soft fibreboard impact-sound insulation
   30 mm layer of stone chippings
   162 mm lam. fir-plank element, layers glued at
   right angles to each other
   28 mm sound insulation, 15 mm plasterboard
3 160 mm lam. fir-plank element,
   layers glued at right angles to each other,
   top layer in larch

4 internal bracing-wall construction:
   12.5 mm plasterboard
   94 mm lam. fir-plank element,
   layers glued at right angles to each other
   50 mm battens
   12.5 mm plasterboard, 8 mm tiling
5 external wall construction:
   19 mm larch boarding
   30 mm battens
   80 mm soft fibreboard insulation
   94 mm lam. fir-plank element,
   layers glued at right angles to each other
   50 mm structure-borne sound insulation
   2× 12.5 mm plasterboard
6 19 mm larch boarding
   30 mm counter-battens, 80 mm battens
   94 mm lam. fir-plank element,
   layers glued at right angles to each other
   19 mm softwood boarding

Housing Development in Dornbirn

Architects: B & E Baumschlager-Eberle, Lochau

This new housing development on the outskirts of Dornbirn, Austria, is hidden behind an old barn on a long, narrow site. It contains seven dwellings and stands out from the traditional, pitched-roofed building fabric by virtue of its unusual volumetric form and facade design. The structure consists of two perpendicularly offset tracts, two and three storeys high respectively. This layout serves to integrate the structure into the small-scale surroundings and to define new external spaces.

In order to fully utilise the narrow site, the building was placed hard on the set-back line and the underground carparking is accessed via the renovated barn construction. The stairwells are centrally located at the junction of the two tracts, providing vertical access to the three apartments with loggias on each of the lower floors; and to the single roof apartment with integrated terrace. All apartments are designed as corner dwellings, thereby being ideally lit and ventilated. The core zones, accommodating the kitchens and bathrooms, are placed adjacent to the access routes of stair and hallway, providing sound buffers.

This cubic complex reacts not only volumetrically, but also visually, to the density of its environment – by reflecting it back from the white glazed facades, which are articulated into horizontal bands by black guide tracks thereby creating an illusion of space. Set out in three planes, the sliding glazing elements lend the smooth surface a subtle sense of depth. The surroundings are also reflected in the glass in different ways: as clearly defined images in the rectangular windows in the wall plane behind the outer layers of glazing, or diffused in the white screen-printed surface. The effect of the facades is dependent upon the continually changing weather conditions, natural lighting and time of day.

Timber stud-walling, with synthetic-resin-bonded laminated timber boarding, is hidden behind the external glass skin. The facade elements provide the necessary degree of privacy, both internally and within the loggias, without impeding views out of the building. The loggias can be easily converted into conservatories as desired, the lighting of which can be altered by the residents by simply sliding the glass panels over each other for a single- or double-layered-effect.

Variability is a predominant part of unified facade concept – the full impact of the homogeneous outer skin being ultimately revealed when the individual elements are in everyday use.

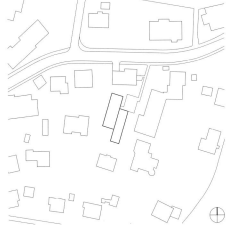

Site plan   scale 1:2500
Sections   scale 1:500

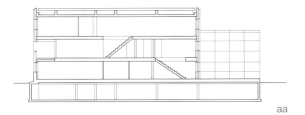

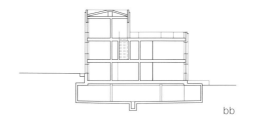

aa

bb

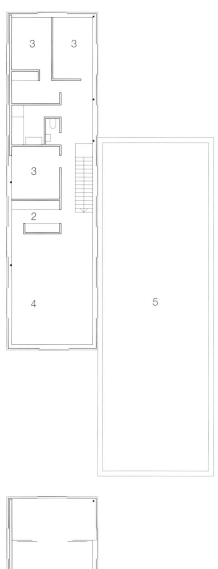

Project details:
Usage: 7 dwelling units
Units: 2× 2-room apartments (48 m²)
                    2× 3-room apartments (70 m²)
                    1× 3-room apartment (87 m²)
                    2× 3-room apartments (102 m²)
Internal room height: 2.38 and 2.80 m
Construction: Timber stud walling with
                    reinforced concrete slabs
Unit access: Multi-dwelling units
Residential area: 692.20 m²
Total site area: 1,302 m²
Construction time: Jun 2000 – Nov 2001

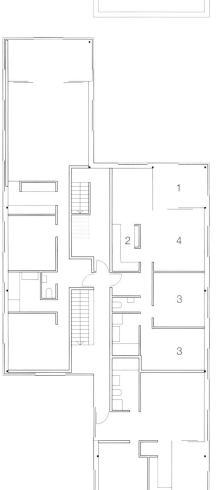

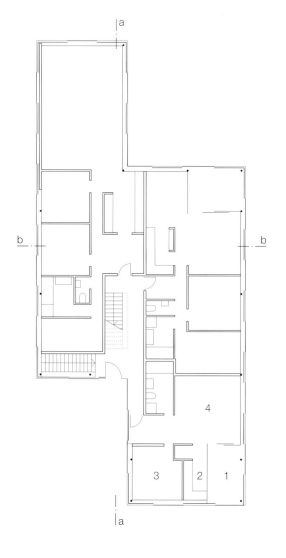

Floor plans
scale 1:2500

1 Loggia
2 Kitchen
3 Bedroom
4 Living room
5 Roof terrace

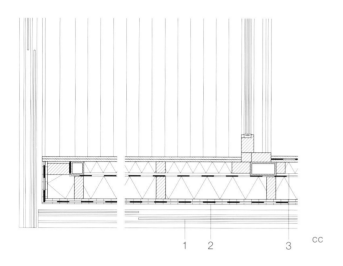

cc

Vertical and horizontal sections
scale 1:20

1 6 mm toughened glass in triple sliding track
   single-colour screen printed with Ø 1 mm dots
2 timber-stud wall:
   5 mm synthetic-resin-bonded laminated wood board
   moisture-diffusing windproof layer, 12 mm OSB
   120 mm thermal insulation lined with building paper
   120/60 mm timber studs
3 internal timber-stud dry lining:
   60 mm thermal insulation
   PE sheet vapour barrier between
   2× 12.5 mm plasterboard
4 powder-coated aluminium section
5 130/90 mm steel angle

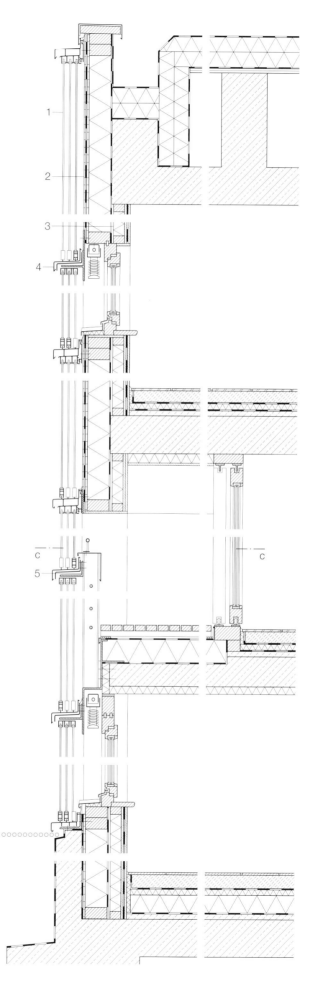

Housing Development in Trofaiach

Architect: Hubert Riess, Graz

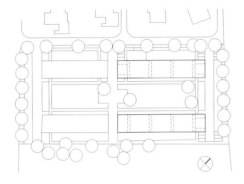

This housing development is found in the township of Trofaiach, 40 km from Graz in Austria. It occupies an entire street block, comprising two three-storey linear tracts with a protected landscaped zone located between them. The strips are each divided by four cascading straight-flight staircases that extend through the full depths of the blocks.

The locations of the staircases are easily recognised in the elevations, via storey-high openings. Each staircase provides access from the courtyard side to two of the eight dwellings on each floor. This type of access caused minor variations in the layouts of the dwellings, the entrances being off-set from each other, while still allowing the locations of the bathrooms to remain consistent fly above each other.

The dwellings themselves have an east-west orientation, and are set back from the courtyard through the use of loggias, which are accessible from two sides. The ground floor dwellings also have private external seating areas to the street frontage.

A high level of prefabrication was used in this project. All external walls and party cross-walls are load-bearing and of timber cross-framing and manufactured in storey-height units. The facade elements are connected by laminated timber beams and fixed to the floors. The roofs and staircases are also of prefabricated unit construction systems. The space under the stairscases is utilised as storage area; the partition walls of which, serve as additional load-bearing elements. The larch facade cladding was executed on site. The generous glazing towards the courtyard side is fixed up to balustrade height, with adjustable timber louvres providing privacy and sun-screening.

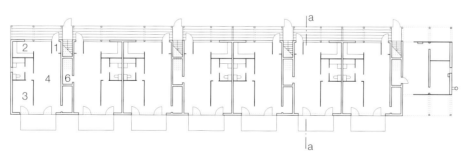

Site plan
scale 1:2500
Floor plans
scale 1:500

1 Entrance
2 Kitchen
3 Room
4 Living room
5 Loggia
6 Store

Diagrams of
prefabricated elements
scale 1:200

1 facade element:
   timber studding
   thermal insulation
   gypsum fibreboard on
   both faces

2 roof element: rafters
   thermal insulation
   chipboard on both faces
3 floor element:
   stacked plank floor
4 laminated timber beam
5 internal wall element:
   timber studding, insulation
   gypsum fibreboard on
   both faces

Project details:
Usage: 45 dwelling units
Units: 13× 2-room apartments (57 m²)
                          32× 3-room apartments (69 m²)
Internal room height: 2.48 m
Construction: Timber cross-framing with stacked floor slabs
Unit access: Double-unit dwelling units
Total floor area: 3,138.91 m²
Total site area: 5,142 m²
Construction time: Mar 1999 – Jul 2000

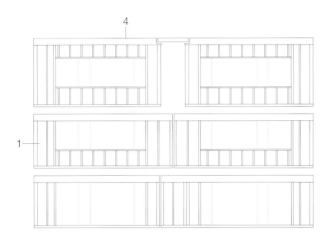

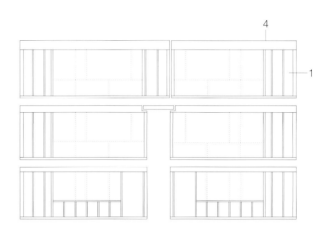

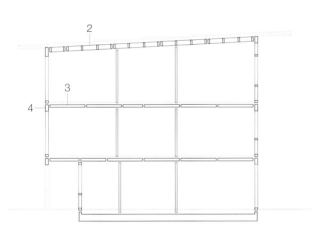

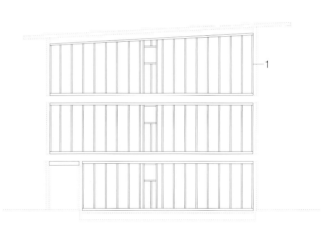

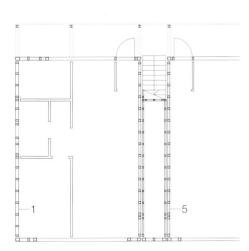

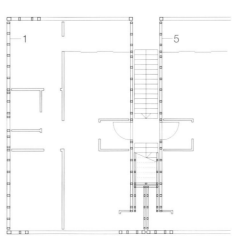

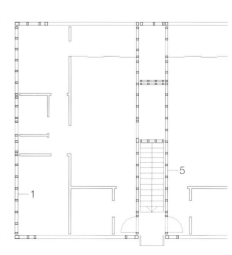

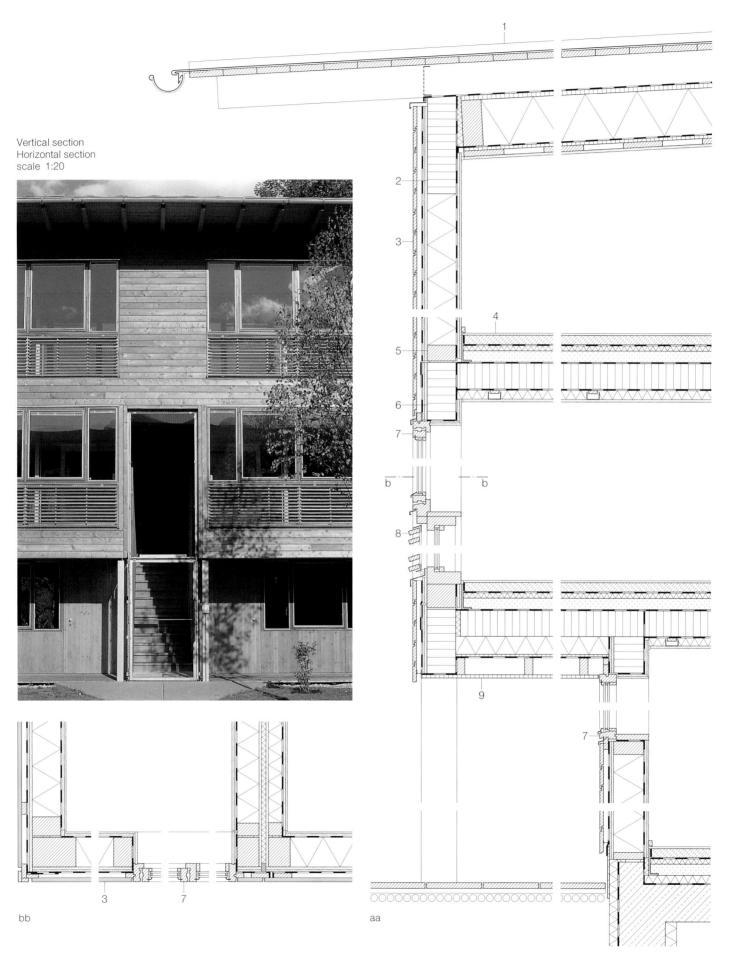

Vertical section
Horizontal section
scale 1:20

1

2

3

4

5

6

7

b   b

8

9

7

bb

3   7

aa

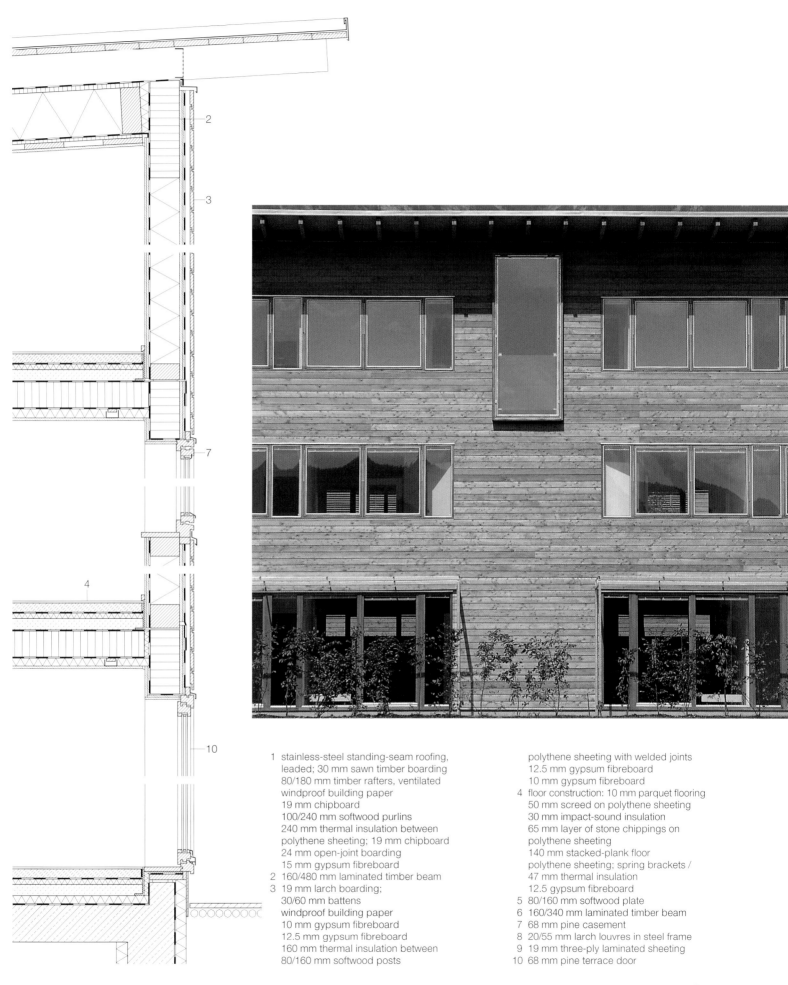

1 stainless-steel standing-seam roofing,
  leaded; 30 mm sawn timber boarding
  80/180 mm timber rafters, ventilated
  windproof building paper
  19 mm chipboard
  100/240 mm softwood purlins
  240 mm thermal insulation between
  polythene sheeting; 19 mm chipboard
  24 mm open-joint boarding
  15 mm gypsum fibreboard
2 160/480 mm laminated timber beam
3 19 mm larch boarding;
  30/60 mm battens
  windproof building paper
  10 mm gypsum fibreboard
  12.5 mm gypsum fibreboard
  160 mm thermal insulation between
  80/160 mm softwood posts

polythene sheeting with welded joints
12.5 mm gypsum fibreboard
10 mm gypsum fibreboard
4 floor construction: 10 mm parquet flooring
  50 mm screed on polythene sheeting
  30 mm impact-sound insulation
  65 mm layer of stone chippings on
  polythene sheeting
  140 mm stacked-plank floor
  polythene sheeting; spring brackets /
  47 mm thermal insulation
  12.5 gypsum fibreboard
5 80/160 mm softwood plate
6 160/340 mm laminated timber beam
7 68 mm pine casement
8 20/55 mm larch louvres in steel frame
9 19 mm three-ply laminated sheeting
10 68 mm pine terrace door

67

Housing Towers in Constance

Architects: Ingo Bucher-Beholz, Gaienhofen

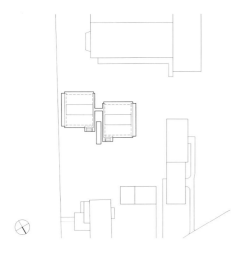

As part of the desired increase in urban density in the town of Constance, two residential towers, off-set from each other, were built on a narrow site. The architects decided upon this scheme in order to maximise the incidence of natural lighting and amount of external space afforded the residents. Access to both levels of the 12 low-cost maisonette dwellings is via external steel staircases and covered galleries. The towers are also linked by steel bridges supporting extensive planting, providing further possible communication zones.

The lower dwellings are two storeys high, while the upper dwellings are three-storeys high and include roof terraces. The covered walkways and balconies extend the living spaces to the east and west. These facades are fully glazed and supplied with awnings, providing the necessary privacy and sun screening. The open-plan layout, based on a four metre grid, orientates the living and sleeping spaces, similarly, to the east and the west. The zoning is determined by the centrally located service and access cores. In the absence of a basement, the blocks are raised above the ground, with the undercroft area providing space for parking, services and storage.

The simple steel structure facilitated the erection of the towers in a low-energy form of construction in only six months. The precast concrete slabs are fixed to the steel framing via stud-shear connectors. All internal and external walls are in non-load-bearing dry construction. Steel beams, columns and wind-bracing elements are housed in the transverse-walls. The only stiffening in the longitudinal direction is provided by the vertical external wind-bracing structures that transmit the loads from the end walls directly to the foundations.

Site plan   scale 1:500
North elevation
Plan of 1st and 3rd floors
Plan of 2nd and 4th floors
Plan of roof storey   scale 1:500

Project Details:
Usage:	12 dwelling units
Units:	10× 3-room apartments (82 m²)
	2× 5-room apartments (106 m²)
Internal room height:	2.30 m
Construction:	Steel frame
Unit access:	Covered access galleries
Total floor area:	1,148 m²
Total site area:	836 m²
Construction time:	May 1995 – Dec 1995

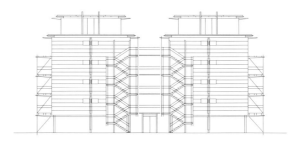

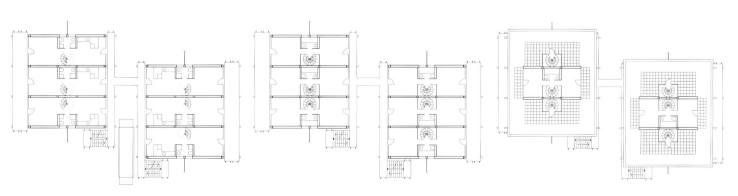

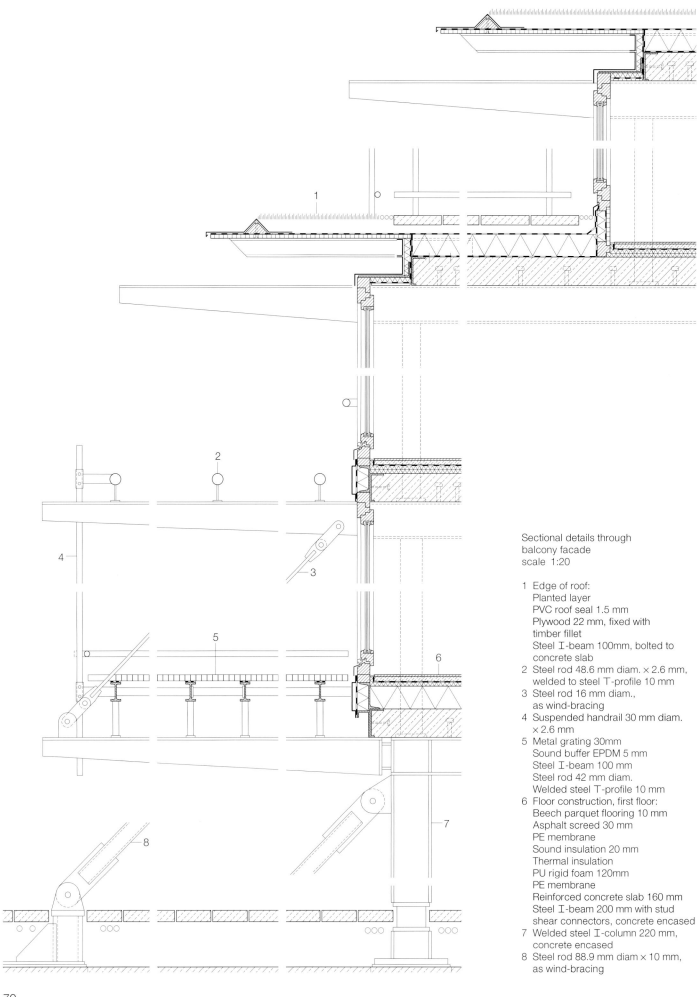

Sectional details through
balcony facade
scale 1:20

1 Edge of roof:
   Planted layer
   PVC roof seal 1.5 mm
   Plywood 22 mm, fixed with
   timber fillet
   Steel I-beam 100mm, bolted to
   concrete slab
2 Steel rod 48.6 mm diam. × 2.6 mm,
   welded to steel T-profile 10 mm
3 Steel rod 16 mm diam.,
   as wind-bracing
4 Suspended handrail 30 mm diam.
   × 2.6 mm
5 Metal grating 30mm
   Sound buffer EPDM 5 mm
   Steel I-beam 100 mm
   Steel rod 42 mm diam.
   Welded steel T-profile 10 mm
6 Floor construction, first floor:
   Beech parquet flooring 10 mm
   Asphalt screed 30 mm
   PE membrane
   Sound insulation 20 mm
   Thermal insulation
   PU rigid foam 120mm
   PE membrane
   Reinforced concrete slab 160 mm
   Steel I-beam 200 mm with stud
   shear connectors, concrete encased
7 Welded steel I-column 220 mm,
   concrete encased
8 Steel rod 88.9 mm diam × 10 mm,
   as wind-bracing

70

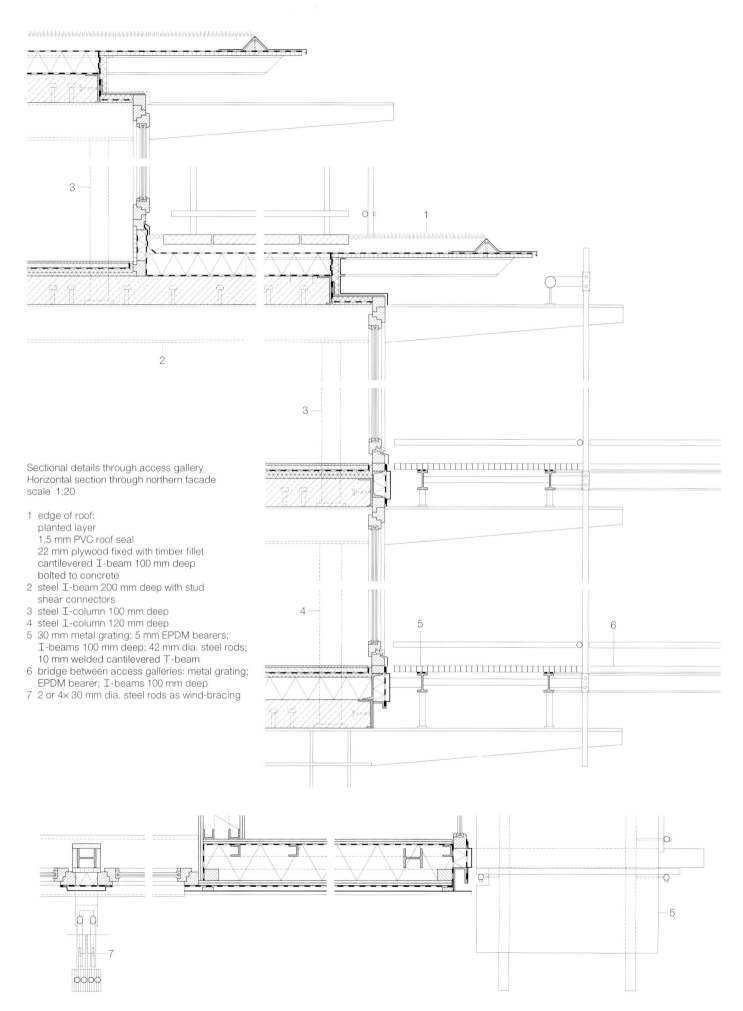

Sectional details through access gallery
Horizontal section through northern facade
scale 1:20

1 edge of roof:
   planted layer
   1.5 mm PVC roof seal
   22 mm plywood fixed with timber fillet
   cantilevered I-beam 100 mm deep
   bolted to concrete
2 steel I-beam 200 mm deep with stud
   shear connectors
3 steel I-column 100 mm deep
4 steel I-column 120 mm deep
5 30 mm metal grating; 5 mm EPDM bearers;
   I-beams 100 mm deep; 42 mm dia. steel rods;
   10 mm welded cantilevered T-beam
6 bridge between access galleries: metal grating;
   EPDM bearer; I-beams 100 mm deep
7 2 or 4× 30 mm dia. steel rods as wind-bracing

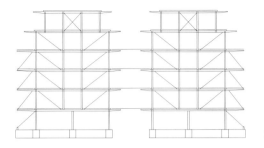

D

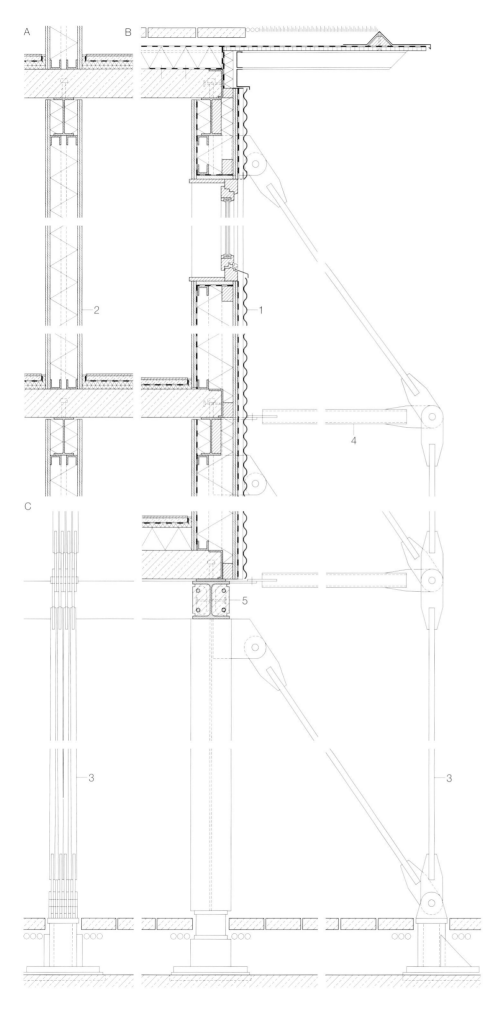

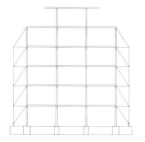

E

A   Section through party wall
B   Section through northern external wall
C   End view of wind bracing
      scale 1:20
D, E Structural system
      scale 1:500

1 wall construction:
    18/76 mm corrugated aluminium sheeting
    30/60 mm battens
    waterproofing layer
    2× 12.5 mm gypsum fibreboard
    185 mm mineral-fibre thermal insulation
    vapour barrier
    plasterboard 2× 12.5 mm
2 party wall construction:
    2× 12.5 mm plasterboard
    150 mm mineral fibre thermal insulation
    2× 12.5 mm plasterboard
3 30 mm dia. steel rod
4 76.1 mm dia. tube 8 mm thick
5 steel I-beam 200 mm deep

Residential and Commercial Centre near Copenhagen

Architects: Arkitektfirmaet C.F. Møller, Copenhagen

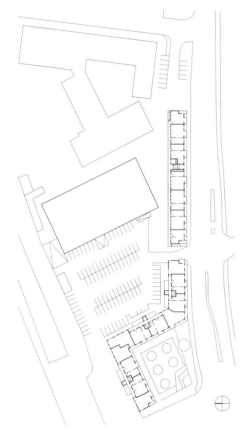

The location of this residential and commercial development in the small Danish town of Bagsværd, 15 km north of Copenhagen, was previously a neglected site overwhelmed by the adjacent railway station, high-rise blocks and the accompanying disastrous wind tunnel effects.

This three and four storey development is ranged along the east-west orientated main road and encloses the newly created plaza. The rear of the building is given over to a new supermarket and its associated carparking requirements.

The third and final building phase will include the renovation of existing retail outlets and the cinema. The footpaths along the main road have been elevated to coincide with the shop front levels under a colonnade which runs the entire length of the building. The ground floor provides space for the retail elements of the project, while the first floor is utilised as office space, and 38 collectively owned residental units complete the development on the upper levels.

Central stairwells and short covered walkways provide access to the apartments, simultaneously offering residents an opportunity for communal seating and meeting areas. All dwellings include either a balcony or bay window looking out over either the street or plaza. The layout of the apartments is based on a linear living and kitchen area accessing both facades, while the bathrooms are relegated to the less desirable core zone of the tracts.

The construction system selected for this project was a mixture of reinforced concrete for the ground floor, a timber-panelled structure for the top storey and steel-framed construction for the intermediate levels. Cantilevered steel bays and balconies, with aluminium-framed glazing on three sides, enhance the natural lighting component of the interiors.

Site plan and second floor plan
scale 1:2000
Vertical section
scale 1:20

Project details:
Usage:	38 dwelling units
Units:	2× 2-room (50 m²)
	3× 4-room (100 m²)
	33× 3-room (85 m²)
Internal room height:	2.50 m
Construction:	Reinforced concrete, steel-framed and timber-panelled construction
Unit access:	Covered walkway
Total floor area:	7,000 m²
Total site area:	2,400 m²
Construction time:	Aug 1999 – Dec 2000

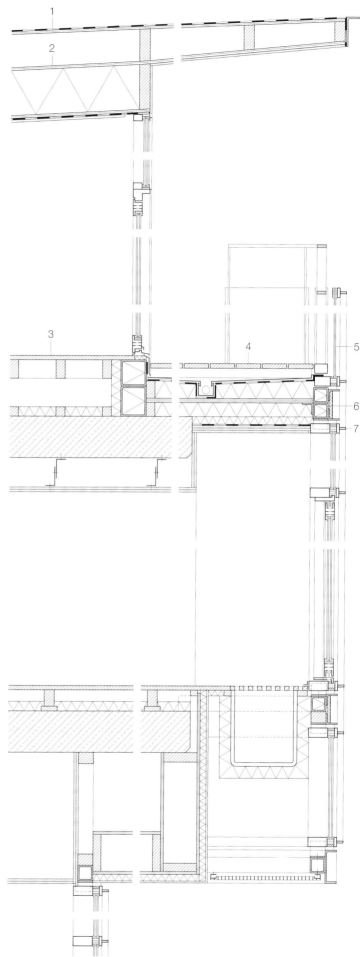

1 Bituminous membrane, double layer
2 Timber slab element with insulation 250 mm
   Vapour barrier, plasterboard 12.5 mm
3 flooring: oakboards 22 mm
   Softwood batten 50 × 100 mm
   Softwood cross battens 50 × 150 mm
   Mineral wool sound insulation 50 mm
   Reinforced concrete slab 220 mm
4 Teak boards 25 × 135 mm
   Aluminium sheeting 2 mm
   Bituminous sheeting, double layer
   Mineral wool thermal insulation with gradient 100 mm
   Waterproof particle board 22 mm
   Thermal insulation 50 mm
   Vapour barrier
   Plasterboard, triple layer 37.5 mm
5 Screen printed safety glass balustrading 10 mm
6 Insulated steel RHS 90 × 90 × 5 mm
7 Aluminium post and beam facade 120 × 50 mm

Housing in Tokyo

Architects: Riken Yamamoto & Field Shop, Yokohama

Project details:

Usage:	420 multiple dwelling units, offices, retail space and kindergarten
Construction:	Reinforced concrete
Residential areas:	42–125 m²
Internal room height:	2.30 m
Unit access:	Centrally accessed apartments
Total floor area:	50,095 m²
Total site area:	9,221 m²
Construction time:	May 2001 – Jul 2003

Site plan   scale 1:4000

This new housing development on Shinonome Canal in Tokyo is located approximately 5 km from the city centre. It is a large-scale development, with a master plan determining not only the urban structure, but also the collaboration of the various planners. The entire project includes six housing blocks from various architects, accommodating 2000 dwellings of high urban density. The ground floor pedestal building – containing various retail and community spaces – is sliced through by an S-shaped, meandering promenade and provides the base construction for the housing blocks above. The first building phase of 420 dwellings, by Riken Yamamoto, includes three housing blocks; one 10-storey block and two 14-storey blocks of reinforced concrete framework construction.

The facades are broken up by colourful, two storey loggias inserted in a seemingly random manner. They provide communal areas for the residents and serve also as light and ventilation sources for the corridors which function as internal streetscapes. The apartments are accessed from both sides of these corridors via large-scale glazed facades. As transition zones between the public thoroughfares and the private dwellings, small communal office spaces have been provided. The dwellings themselves are compact in their layout and constructed of plasterboard internal walling while permanent wall cupboards provide the necessary storage alternatives. A single unit kitchen and bathroom cell is placed on the external facade, whereby the glass dividing partitions allow sufficient natural lighting to penetrate the apartments. All glass elements can be screened with either opaque or translucent sliding panels, thereby providing control over the internal environment on a personal basis. Over 100 different apartment layouts enable all individual requirements of the residents to be met.

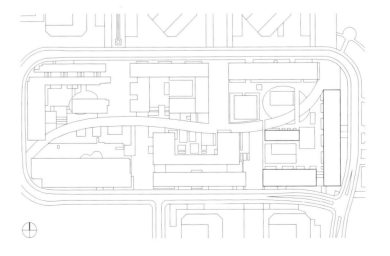

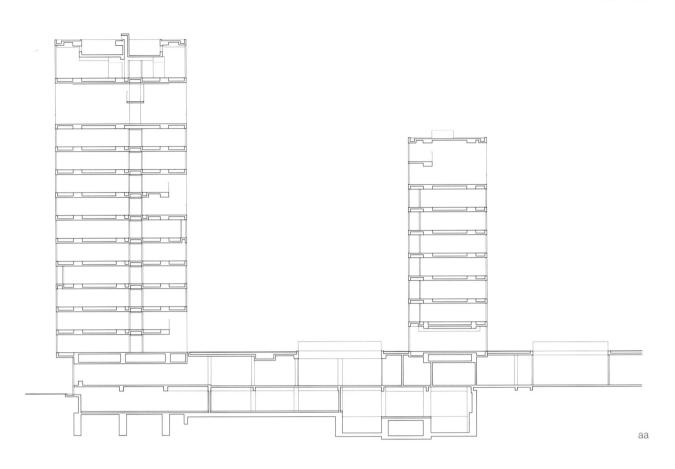

aa

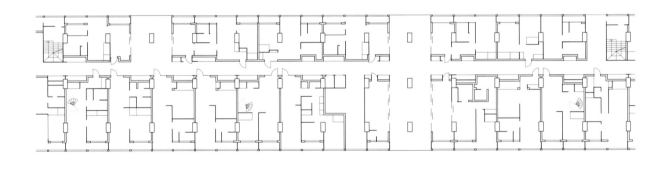

a

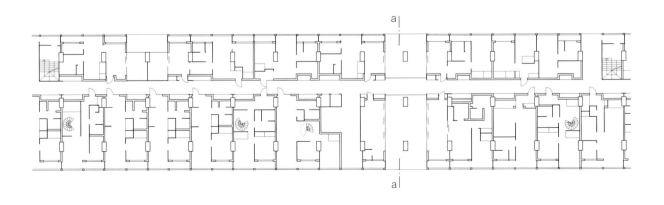

a

Housing Blocks in Gifu

Architects: Kazuyo Sejima and Associates, Tokyo

Project details:
Usage: 107 dwelling units
Construction: Reinforced concrete
Floor areas: 30 apartment types
                             49–80 m²
Internal room height: 2.30 and 5.22 m
Unit access: Covered walkway apart-
                             ments
Total floor area: 4706 m² (1st stage)
                             4755 m² (2nd stage)
Construction time: 1994–1998 (1st stage)
                             1998–2000 (2nd stage)

Site plan   scale 1:5000

The designs of these public housing schemes, on the fringe of the Japanese city of Gifu, by Kazuyo Sejima and Associates are part of a programme based on an idea from and developed by Arata Isozaki. The folded linear blocks, located peripherally on the sites, are four structurally discrete elements and accommodate 107 dwellings. The buildings are long and narrow to facilitate cross-ventilation in the hot humid summers. The dwellings are entered via access balconies reaching every level along the north faces, while striking galvanized steel staircases extend over the full height of the two buildings, enlivening the somewhat repetitive grid structures of the facades. Officially, the stairs serve merely as escape routes and zones of communication, since the lifts are the main form of vertical circulation. The outer faces of the access balconies, clad in expanded wire mesh, have a translucent quality. Punched-out "window gaps" at irregular intervals in the access balconies relieve the elevations, while providing private terraces for individual dwellings. Within the rigid cross-wall construction, with minimal span – one room module corresponding to the axis grid – a multitude of almost identical room-cells has been produced while a remarkable range of 30 different dwelling layouts over ten storeys has been achieved by combining these modules in an apparently random fashion. A third of all dwellings are, in fact, maisonettes via the horizontal connections of room units, while approximately one half are provided with double-storey high spaces. In all apartments, however, the rooms are spread along the south facade adjacent to glazed walkways. Each dwelling is provided with at least one traditional Japanese room, one bedroom, a kitchen and a terrace. Further internal access zones exist within all the dwellings along the south facade, accessed through generous door openings.

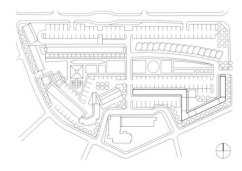

Floor plans, first to fourth floors
scale 1:400

Sectional development
scale 1:1000

1 Terrace
2 Hallway
3 Kitchen
4 Bedroom
5 Traditional Japanese room
6 Gallery space

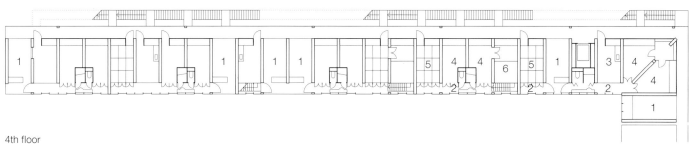

4th floor

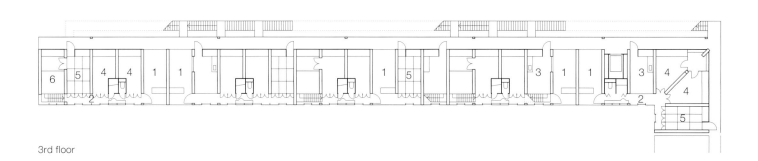

3rd floor

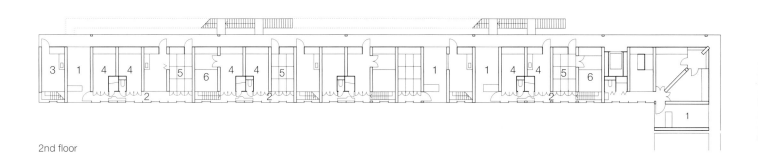

2nd floor

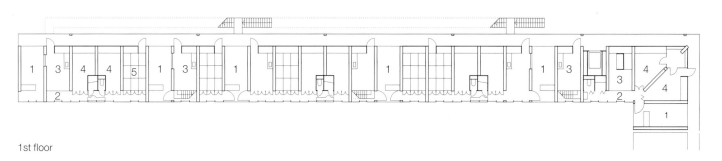

1st floor

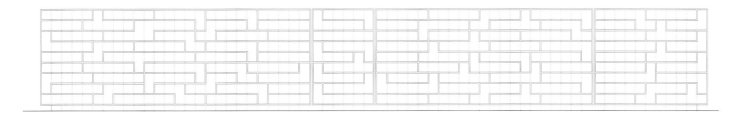

Patio Houses in Amsterdam

Architects: MAP Arquitectos, Josep Lluís Mateo, Barcelona

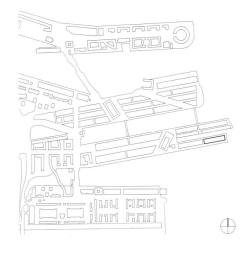

Site plan   scale 1:10000

Josep Lluís Mateo's new compact, elongated, housing development at the head of the Borneo Peninsula resembles a luxury liner lying at anchor in the exclusive former harbour of Amsterdam. The closed volume comprises 26 narrow terraced houses of eleven differing floor plans, varying between 110 and 180 m². The dwellings are laid out back-to-back in a tight scheme which produces a very high density. The construction is a combination of load-bearing, in-situ concrete ballast, with prefabricated floor slabs and facade elements. The entire site area is built over, while the two upper floors are hollowed out producing small private courtyards, gardens and roof terraces to create a richly varied roofscape. The underground garage is sunk by one metre, thereby raising the south-facing dwellings 1.35 m above street level. The parking spaces are situated under only half the area of the north-facing dwellings, allowing the

entrance and rooms facing the street to have an internal room height of 3.50 m. Each dwelling is provided with direct access from the street, from the underground car parking, and internally via stairs; and depending upon location, various green-zones. The south-facing houses have a veranda at street level, a patio on the first floor and a roof terrace. The houses on the opposite side (north-facing), however, may be seen as an introverted housing type. Here the patios, on either the first or second storey, and additional green-zones are all internal. The east-facing dwellings have various different floor plans but all open onto a third floor terrace, the prefabricated glass block flooring panels of which allow daylight to penetrate down into the underlying areas. Various paving solutions have been applied to these outdoor zones according to location; in the gardens the top layer is soil, the terraces are finished with either concrete pavers or

timber decking, and the roof terraces with gravel. The development has two different external images. To the south, the facades are of Canadian red cedar timber panelling, which will gradually weather to grey, lending a restrained maritime character; while to the north, the massive brickwork facades have a somewhat heavy appearance. The wall constructions behind these external finishes, however, are identical. This being a system of prefabricated, thermally insulated timber frame panels, fixed to the edges of the walls and floor slabs, and stabilised internally with plasterboard and externally with particleboard. Window elements of various systems and openings are alternatively hidden behind, or revealed alongside, the timber louvres of the south elevation, creating even more interest in the play of space and light, in what could otherwise have become a standardized facade.

Floor plans   Sections   scale 1:500

A Basement
B Ground floor
C First floor
D Second floor

Project details:

Usage:	26 dwelling units
Units:	4 variations south-facing 111–136 m²
	3 variations north-facing 118–175 m²
	4 variations east-facing 131–181 m²
Internal room height:	2.70–3.50 m
Construction:	Reinforced concrete
Unit access:	Single access dwellings
Total floor area:	7,205 m²
Total site area:	3,500 m²
Open space:	1,030 m²
Construction time:	1996–2000

aa

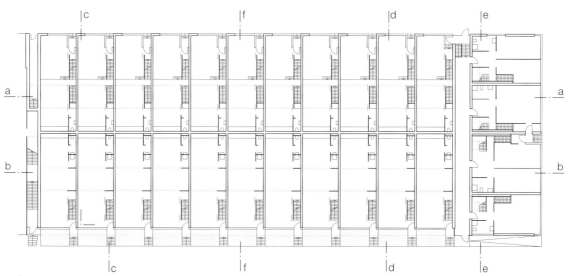

B

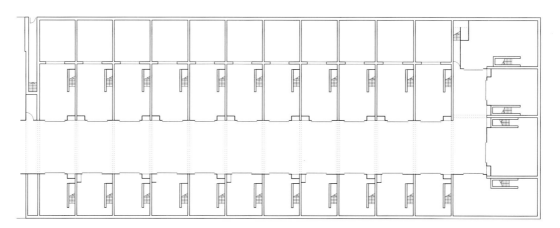

A

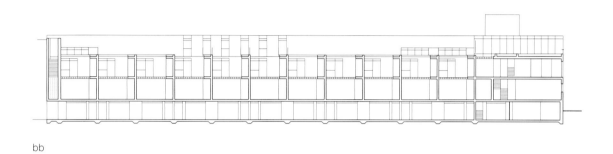

cc

dd

ee

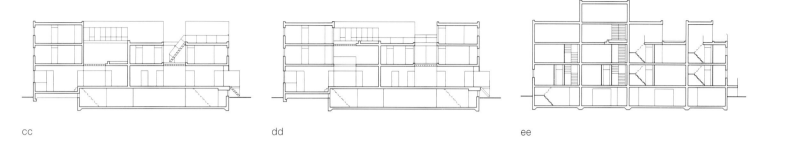

bb

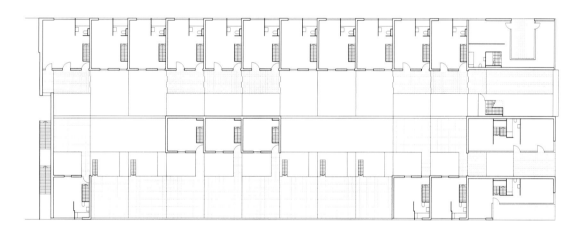

D

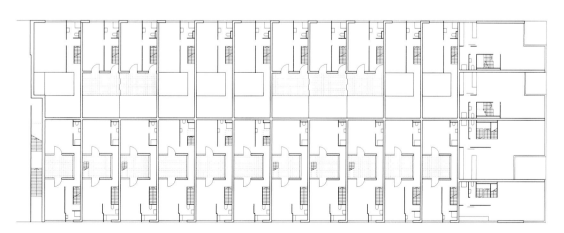

C

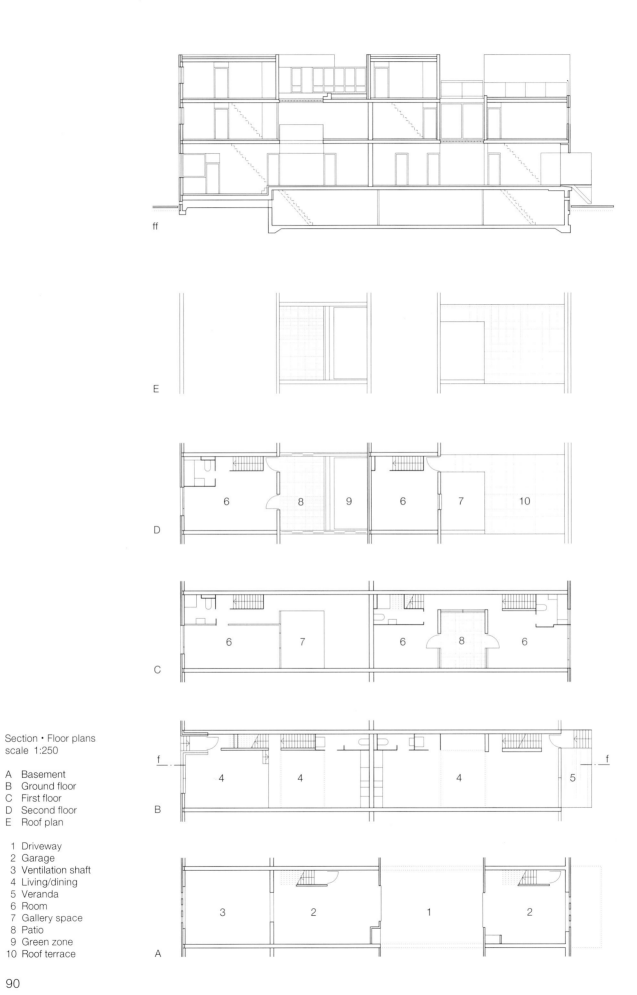

ff

E

D

| 6 | 8 | 9 | 6 | 7 | 10 |

C

| 6 | 7 | 6 | 8 | 6 |

Section · Floor plans
scale 1:250

A Basement
B Ground floor
C First floor
D Second floor
E Roof plan

 1 Driveway
 2 Garage
 3 Ventilation shaft
 4 Living/dining
 5 Veranda
 6 Room
 7 Gallery space
 8 Patio
 9 Green zone
10 Roof terrace

f   f

B

| 4 | 4 | 4 | 5 |

| 3 | 2 | 1 | 2 |

A

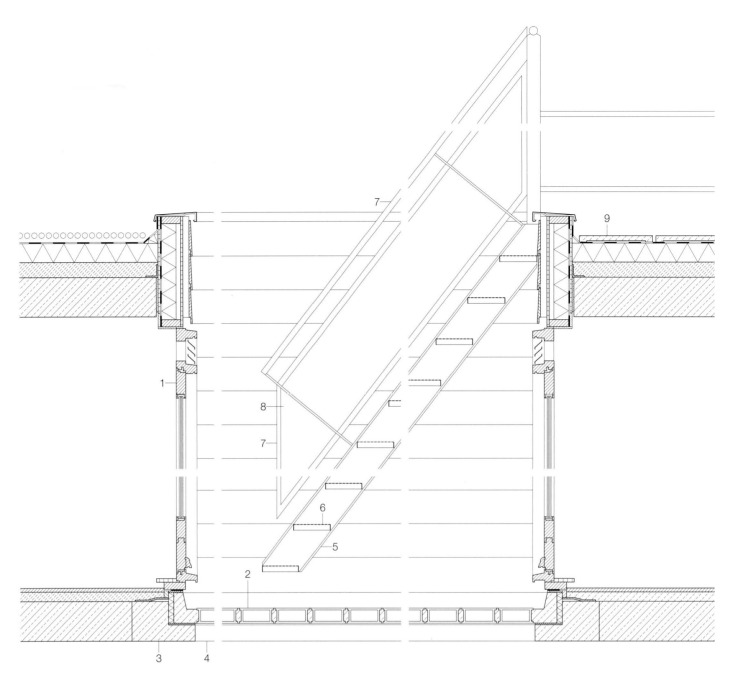

Wall section
Patio and south facade
scale 1:20

1 Iroko timber door
  frame 67 × 114 mm
2 Prefabricated glass
  block panel in
  concrete frame
  3300 × 2100 mm
3 Prefabricated
  reinforced concrete
  edge beam
  350 × 210 mm
4 Steel RHS
  85 × 85 mm
5 Steel channel
  220 mm
6 Profiled steel stair
  treads with turned
  edges
7 Galv. steel profile
  frame and rail
8 Polycarb. panel 10 mm
9 Concrete pavers
  400 × 400 × 30 mm
  Bituminous sheeting
  separation layer
  Rigid foam thermal
  insulation 100 mm

Concrete screed
20–80 mm
Prefabricated
reinforced concrete
slab 210 mm
10 Cedar boarding
  18 mm
  Batten 38 × 38 mm
  Windproof mem-
  brane, Particle-
  board 9 mm
  Thermal insulation
  80 mm, Vapour bar-
  rier, Plasterboard
  12.5 mm
11 Parquet flooring
  20 mm
  Concrete screed
  50 mm
  Prefabricated rein-
  forced concrete
  slab 210 mm
12 Steel RHS
  38 × 38 mm
13 Steel T-section
  38 × 30 mm
14 Timber spacer
  33 × 38 mm
15 Timber 10 mm
16 HEB 140 steel profile

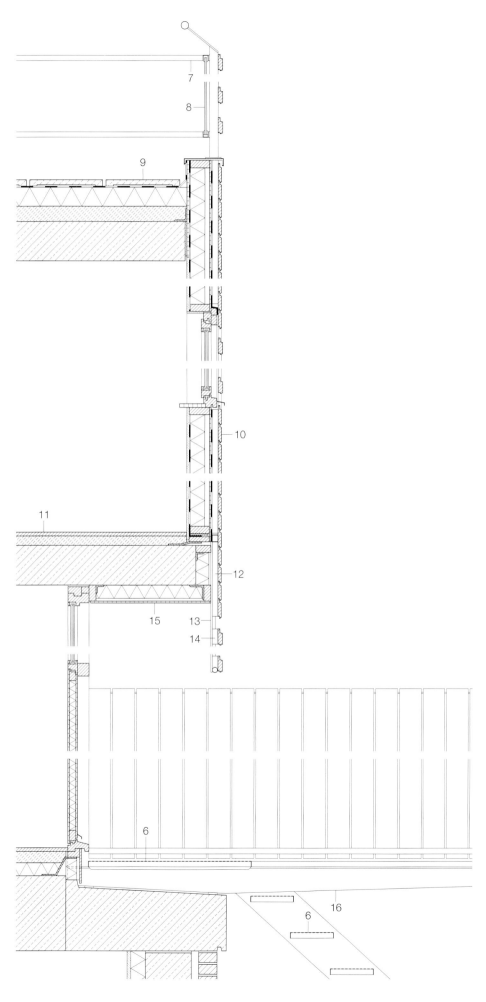

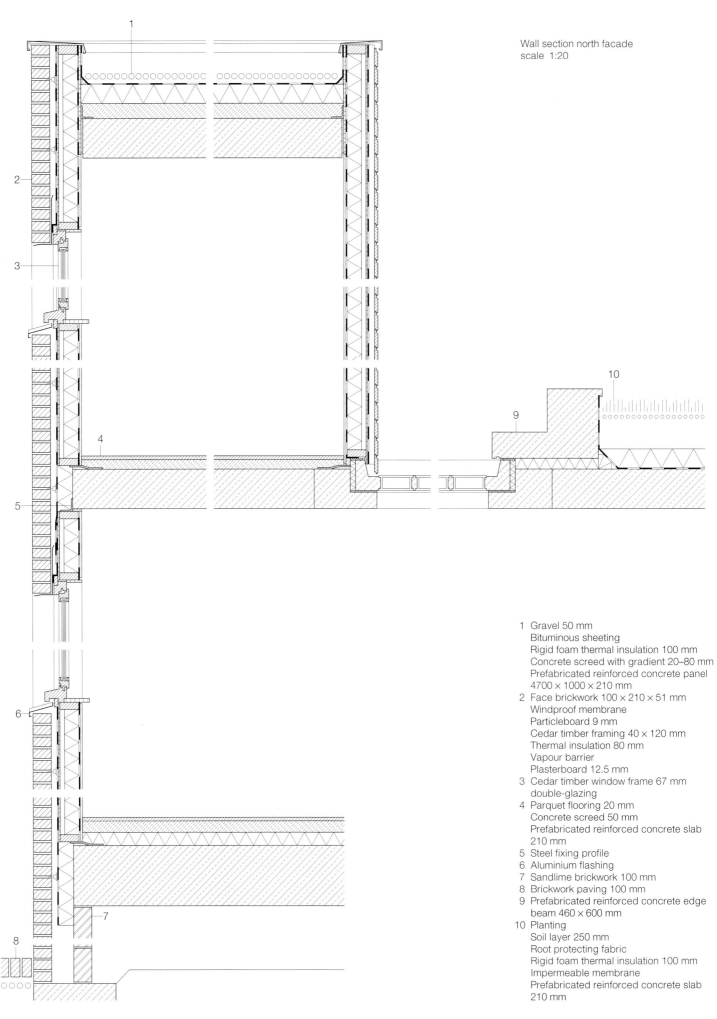

Wall section north facade
scale 1:20

1 Gravel 50 mm
  Bituminous sheeting
  Rigid foam thermal insulation 100 mm
  Concrete screed with gradient 20–80 mm
  Prefabricated reinforced concrete panel
  4700 × 1000 × 210 mm
2 Face brickwork 100 × 210 × 51 mm
  Windproof membrane
  Particleboard 9 mm
  Cedar timber framing 40 × 120 mm
  Thermal insulation 80 mm
  Vapour barrier
  Plasterboard 12.5 mm
3 Cedar timber window frame 67 mm
  double-glazing
4 Parquet flooring 20 mm
  Concrete screed 50 mm
  Prefabricated reinforced concrete slab
  210 mm
5 Steel fixing profile
6 Aluminium flashing
7 Sandlime brickwork 100 mm
8 Brickwork paving 100 mm
9 Prefabricated reinforced concrete edge
  beam 460 × 600 mm
10 Planting
  Soil layer 250 mm
  Root protecting fabric
  Rigid foam thermal insulation 100 mm
  Impermeable membrane
  Prefabricated reinforced concrete slab
  210 mm

Housing Development in Paris

Architects: Herzog & de Meuron, Basel

Project details:
Usage: 57 dwelling units
Construction: Reinforced concrete
                        frame
Floor areas: 33x apartments
                            (47–96 m²)
                        7x lofts
                            (48–75 m²)
                        15x courtyard apartments
                            (70–109 m²)
                        2x cottages
                            (48 m²)
Internal room height: 2.50 m
Unit access: single, double and
                        multi-dwelling units
Total site area: 2,734 m²
Total floor area: 8,419 m²
Construction time: 1999–2000

Folded metal screening now closes the previously incomplete streetscape of the typical 19th century facades in Paris's 14th Arrondissement. The screens mark the recent increase in living density of this 2,700 m² site, which stretches deep into the interior behind neighbouring courtyards. A large range of various dwelling types reflect the mixed living situations of the residents, from street-frontage apartments through to individual lofts and compact family dwellings, providing appropriate accommodation for singles, couples and young families. The street frontages are closed to the outside world by two concrete-framed constructions. The larger of which provides 7 floors with a total of 33 apartments. The folded aspect of the metal facade is carried to its logical conclusion in the planning of the apartments, which are situated facing either the street or courtyard in reflected floor plans of either two or three room designs. Each storey also has a four-room-apartment stretching through to both sides of the building. Narrow balconies run the length of the building between glass facades and the perforated aluminium sheet screening.

The second street frontage is closed by a smaller building providing 7 small single storey lofts of 48 to 75 m² floor area. The central circular stairwell also functions as a room divider in the generous living and dining areas of the dwellings; the bedrooms are located towards the quieter courtyard side of the development. Pedestrian access to the courtyard and underground carparking access are provided adjacent to the slightly elevated ground floor dwellings of both buildings. A row of three to five room apartments are to be found within the elongated courtyard, running parallel to the high stone walls of the neighbouring sites. They are organised in a maisonette fashion, each two apartments sharing a central staircase. Exclusive to the ground floor plans, small concrete "lean-to's" house the kitchens and bathrooms, also creating additional small private internal courtyards. These dwellings open southwards to balconies enclosed by flowing timber-louvred screening, achieving an attractive extension to the living areas. The linear aspect of this large landscaped courtyard is broken up by the two, two-room cottages built hard against the southern wall.

The external exposed concrete walls of these buildings all have plant climbing frames applied to encourage the natural greening of the site in addition to the landscaping.

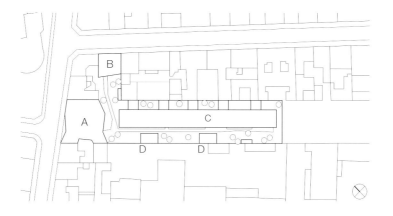

Site plan   scale 1:2000

A Single-storey apartments
B Lofts
C Single-storey apartments
D Cottages

Floor plans   scale 1:750

A Second floor
B First floor
C Ground floor

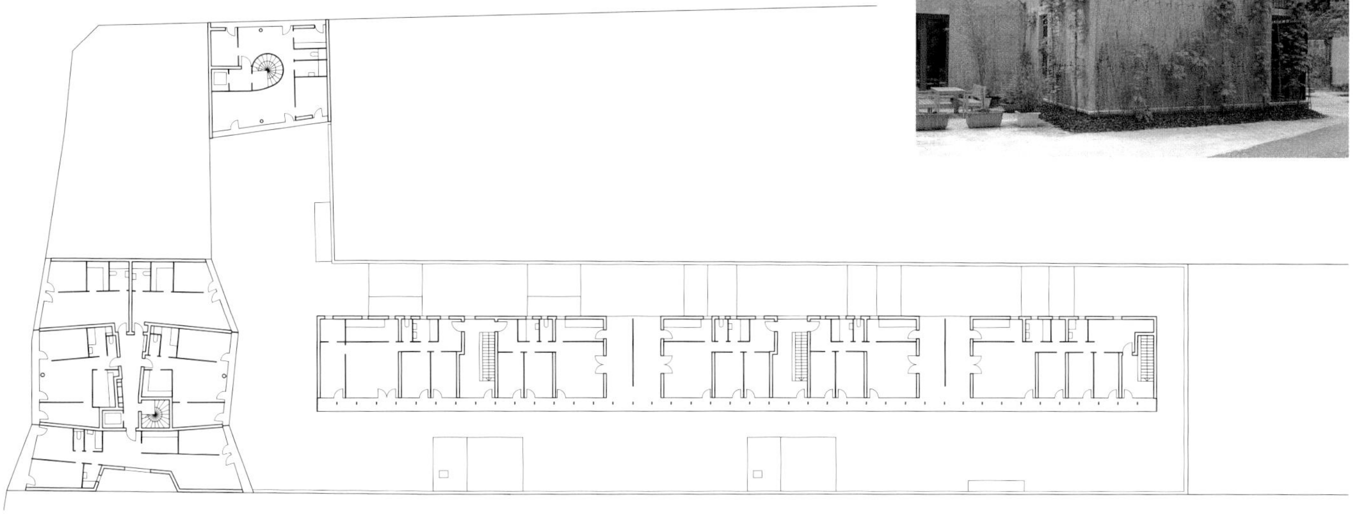

A

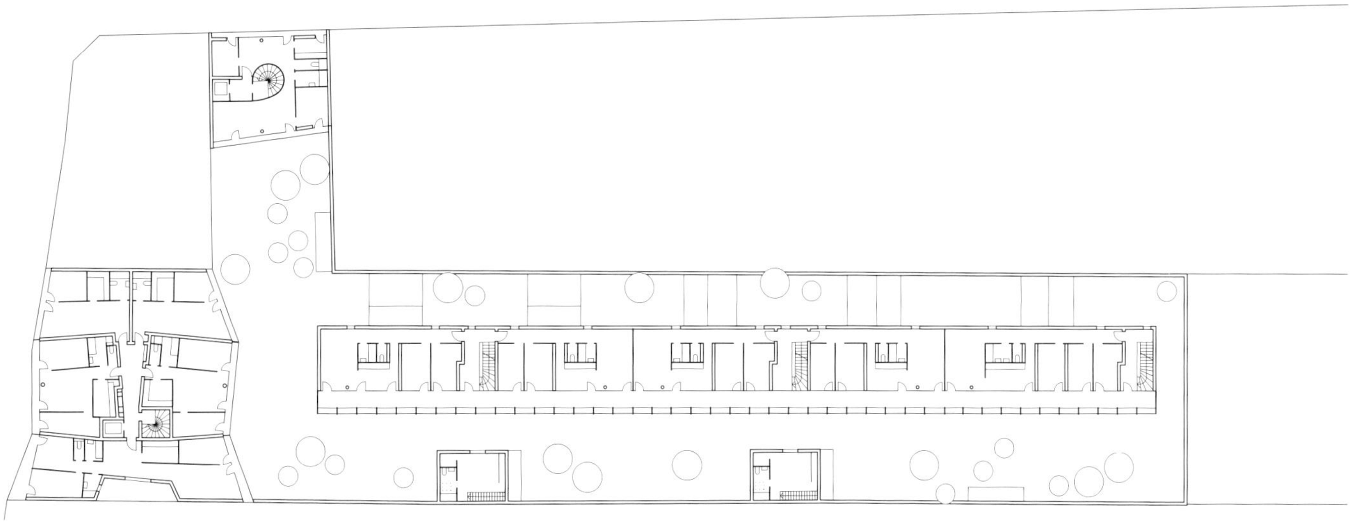

B

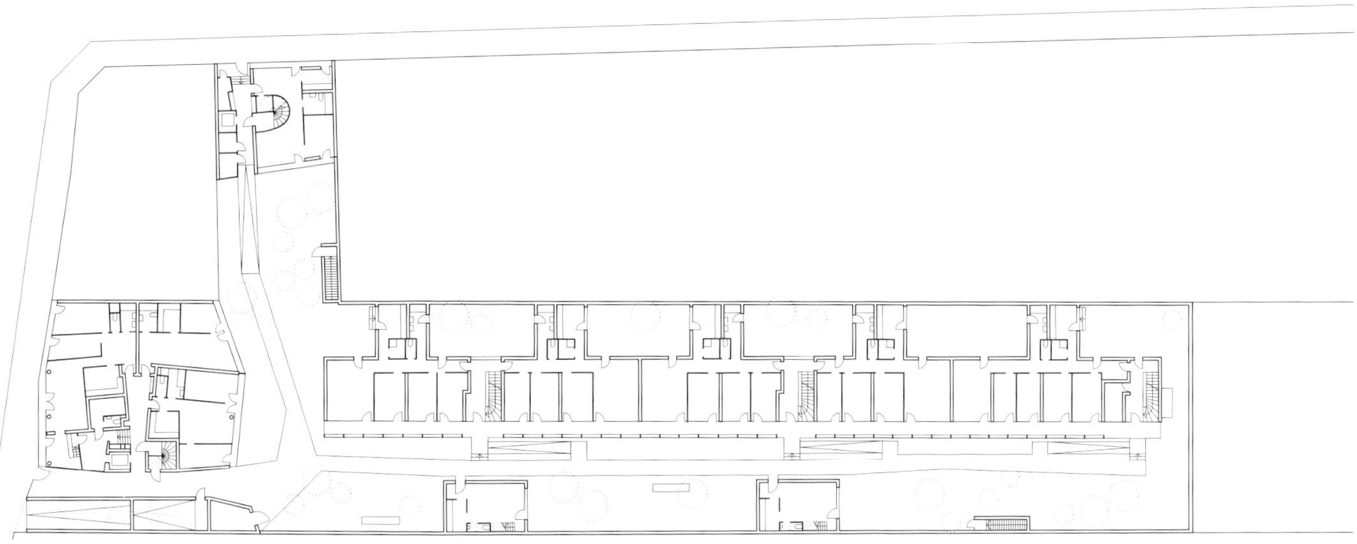

C

Section balcony façade   scale 1:20

1 Roof construction:
 Planting 80 mm
 Bituminous sheeting, double layer
 Thermal insulation 100 mm
 Vapour barrier
 Reinforced concrete slab 180 mm
2 Bituminous sheeting with gradient
3 Timber panelling
4 Moabi timber window frame
 with double glazing
5 Oregon pine timber louvred shuttering
 with 8 mm jointing
6 Aluminium guiding track
7 Balcony construction:
 Timber decking 22 mm, 1% gradient
 Battens 30–50 mm
 Rubber layer 5 mm
 Reinforced concrete slab 180 mm
8 Balustrade:
 Steel handrail 45 × 12 mm
 Steel post 30 × 20 mm
 Steel slats 16 × 16 mm
 Steel rod 30 × 30 mm
9 Floor construction:
 Timber parquet flooring 20 mm
 Screed 50 mm
 Reinforced concrete slab 200 mm
10 Stair/ramp reinforced concrete

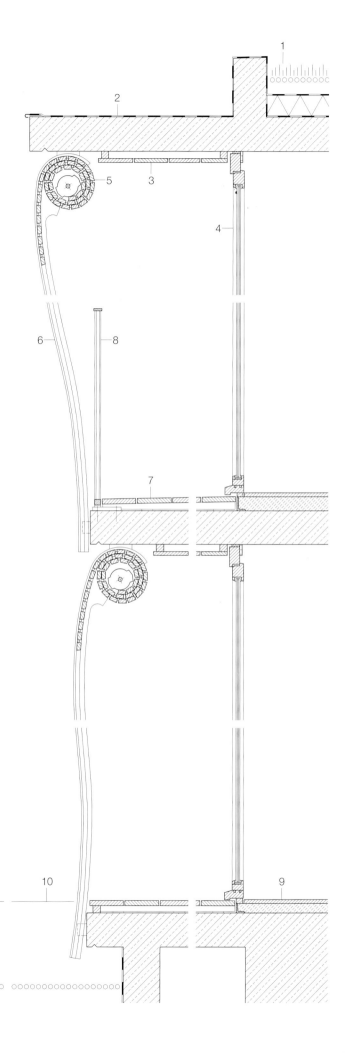

Housing Block in Munich

Architects: meck architekten, Munich

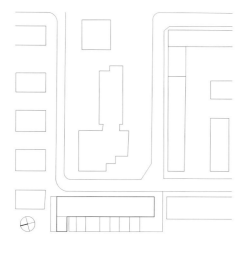

Project details:
Usage: 43 dwelling units
Units: 24× 2-room (57.5 m²)
9× 3-room (75.5 m²)
10× 4-room (94.8 m²)
Internal room height: Ground and 4th floor
2.86 m
1st, 2nd and 3rd floor
2.52 m
Construction: Reinforced concrete
Unit access: Covered walkway
accessed dwellings
Total site area: 2,841 m²
Total floor area: 3,647 m²
Residential area: 2,990 m²
Construction time: Oct 2002 – Jan 2004

Site plan   scale 1:2500
Floor plans   scale 1:500

This publicly funded project was designed to create a new living quarter on the site of a former army base south of Munich's Olympic park – it includes dwellings, a public park, a playground, community facilities, commercial and retail areas. The five storey residential tract accommodates 43 threshhold-free dwellings and abuts directly onto the neighbouring green zone. Interestingly, in the almost 70 metre long building the nine apartments per storey are served by only two single-flight staircases, located against the eastern facade, and minimal covered walkways. The larger 3 and 4-room apartments are located at the ends of these walkways, while the 2-room apartments are placed centrally, with kitchen and bathroom units placed parallel to the walkways, acting as sound buffers for the residents. The living and bedroom areas are orientated westward and take up the entire facade width, accessing the generously planned loggias to varying depths – this layout enables the living rooms to receive additional natural lighting via their glazed corners. The ground floor dwellings each have a terrace and private garden.

The garden elevation is determined by the white rendered framing running around the darker recessive anthracite-coloured balconies and loggias, which in turn provide a background for the daily life being played at by the residents of the development. Orange awnings, which can be totally retracted, are principal elements here, enabling the residents to individually control their environments and allowing a random play of colour. The street frontage elevation is more severely treated, with strong horizontal fenestration bands set within the white rendered facade. The clear, refined image of the building is further enhanced by the careful detailing of junctions and balustrading.

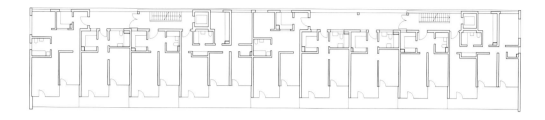

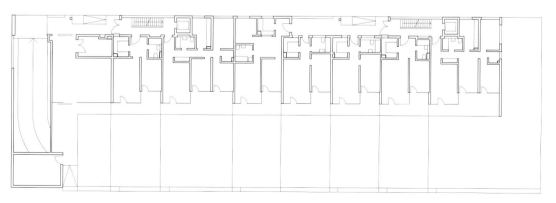

Loggia
Horizontal section · Vertical section
scale 1:20

1 Aluminium sheeting with 5° gradient,
  folded five times
  Fixing element for steel sheeting
  Timber piece on laminated
  plywood panel 19 mm
2 Vegetation 80 mm
  Separation layer
  Thermal insulation140 mm
  Bituminous sheeting, double layer
  Reinforced concrete slab with gradient
3 Joint sealant tape
4 Render 10 mm
  Rigid foam thermal insulation 40 mm
  Reinforced concrete 150–200 mm
5 Steel angle 100 × 100 × 8 mm
6 Timber studs 60 mm
7 Vertical awning
8 Cement-bonded sheeting 12.5 mm,
  exposed surface filled
9 Insulated glazing in timber casement
10 Fibre-cement panel 8 mm
  Cavity 25 mm
  Thermal insulation 80 mm
  Reinforced concrete wall 200 mm
11 Precast reinforced concrete element 300 mm
  Thermally separated steel
  reinforcement connection
12 Balcony partitation
  Fibre-cement panel 8 mm,
  on steel RHS framing 60 × 60 mm
13 Flat steel 40 × 8 mm
  Balustrade post 40 x 8 mm
  Flat steel 35 × 8 mm
  Steel top piece 10mm
14 Prefabricated parquet flooring 10 mm
  Concrete screed 60 mm
  Separation layer
  Sound insulation 30 mm
  Thermal insulation 20 mm (upper floors),
  70 mm (ground floor)
15 Artificial (cast) stone 350 × 350 × 40 mm,
  in gravel bed
16 Galvanized steel gutter

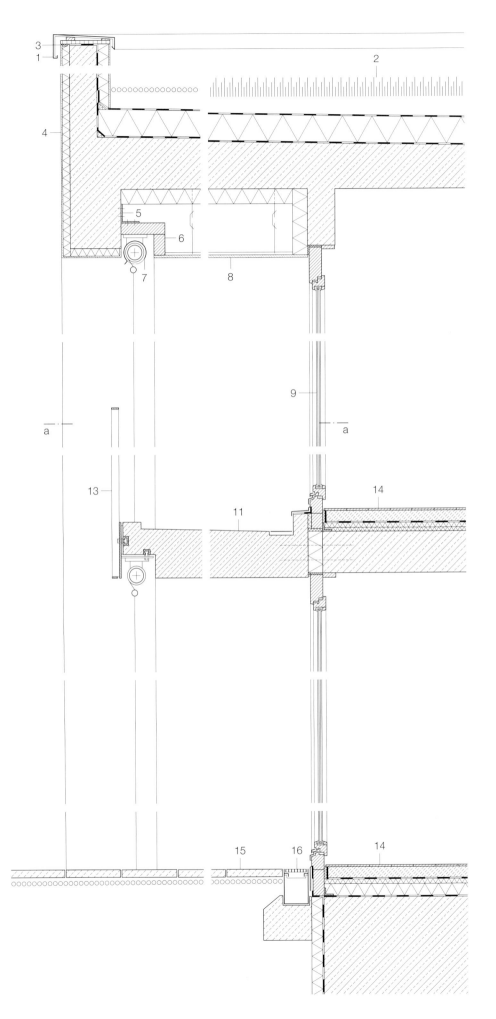

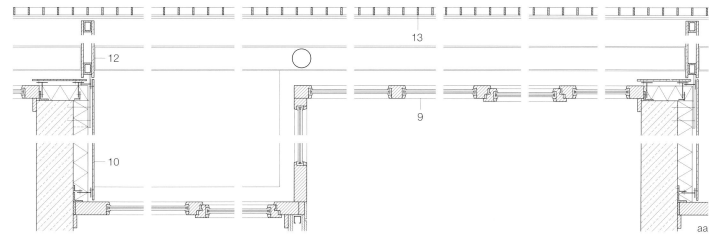

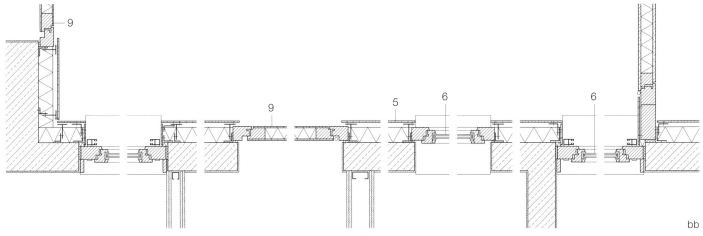

bb

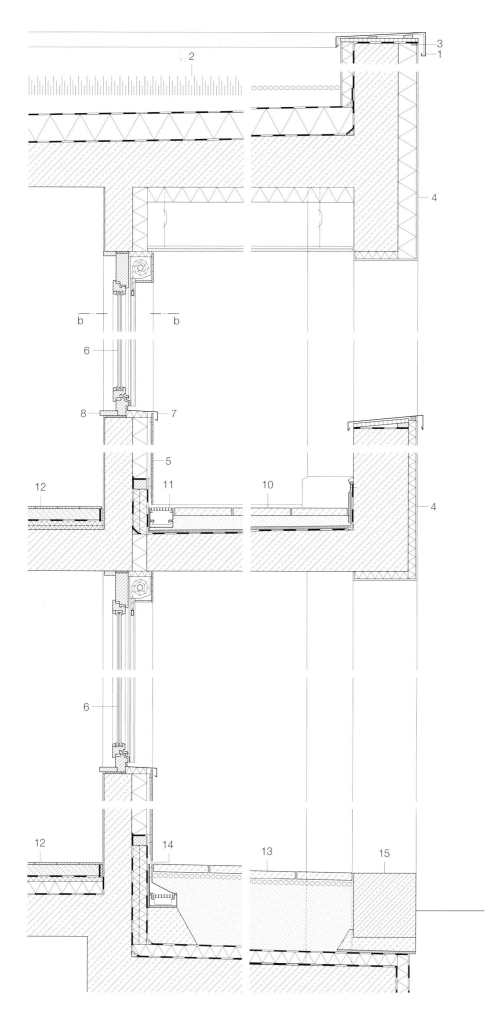

Covered walkway
Horizontal section · Vertical section
scale 1:20

1 Aluminium sheeting with 5° gradient,
  folded five times
  Fixing element for steel sheeting
  Timber piece on 19 mm laminated
  plywood panel
2 Vegetation 80 mm
  Separation layer
  Thermal insulation 140 mm
  Bituminous sheeting, double layer
  Reinforced concrete slab with gradient
  Thermal insulation 80 mm
  Cement-bonded sheeting 12.5 mm,
  exposed surface filled
3 Joint sealant tape
4 Render 10 mm
  Rigid foam thermal insulation 100 mm
  (40 mm balustrading)
  Reinforced concrete wall 240 mm
  (300 mm balustrading)
5 Fibre-cement panel 8 mm
  Cavity 25 mm
  Thermal insulation 80 mm
  Reinforced concrete wall 150–200 mm
6 Insulated glazing in timber casement
7 Aluminium external window sill
8 MDF internal window sill 25 mm
9 Timber door framing
10 Artificial (cast) stone 350 × 350 × 40 mm
   Gravel bed 60–70 mm
   Protective sheeting 5 mm, double layer
   Bituminous roof sheeting, double layer
   Reinforced concrete slab
11 Galvanized steel gutter
12 Prefabricated parquet flooring 10 mm
   Concrete screed 60 mm
   Separation layer
   Sound insulation 30mm
   Thermal insulation 20 mm (upper floors),
   70 mm (ground floor)
13 Artificial (cast) stone 350 × 350 × 40 mm,
   in gravel bed
   Gravel layer 320 mm
   Separation layer
   Perimeter insulation 60 mm
   Bituminous roof sheeting, double layer
   Reinforced concrete slab with gradient
14 Galvanized steel gutter
15 Pre-cast reinforced concrete element,
   350 × 350 mm
   Mortar bed
   Filter mat 12 mm

Two Housing Blocks in Munich

Architects: Rohnke Hild and K, Munich

The new residential quarter in inner-city Munich of Theresien-höhe emerged from an urban planning competition for the site of the former international trade fair halls. On the southern edge of this site are the two five-storey housing blocks by architects Rohnke Hild and K; instantly recognisable by the saw-tooth elements running vertically through the grey facades and above the loggias.

The streetscape here is defined by the site-boundary plan-ning, while the off-set nature of the layout creates a semi-private courtyard area between the two blocks, which sub-sequently merges with the public green zone.

As a result of the U-shaped design of the buildings, the archi-tects have managed to produce a highly desirable range of internal layouts, whereby almost all dwellings are either corner apartments or extend through the building to two facades.

The units range from 1-room apartments to 4-room family dwellings. The bedrooms are spread around the central living area, with loggia and open-plan kitchen placed at opposite ends. This technique enables even the larger dwellings to function well with minimum space wasted on corridors.

An increase of natural daylight has been achieved through corner glazing and the stepping of the facades adjacent to the loggias, further enhanced by 20 cm set-backs in the facades. The loggias are of prefabricated reinforced concrete and con-nected to thermally insulated steel fixings to reduce heat loss; they were subsequently rendered on site.

Standard
floor layout
scale
1:1000

Floor plan
variations
scale
1:500

A 1-room
36 m²
B 3-room
70 m²
C 4-room
80 m²
D 4-room
85 m²
E 4-room
95 m²

Project details:

Usage:	85 dwelling units and 1 community room
Units:	27× 1-room apartments (34–37m²)
	5× 2-room apartments (55–57 m²)
	21× 3-room apartments (60–70 m²)
	36× 4-room apartments (80–95 m²)
Internal room height:	2.50 m
Construction:	Reinforced concrete
Unit access:	Multi-unit dwellings
Residential area:	5,715 m²
Total floor area:	7,299 m²
Total site area:	4,572 m²
Construction time:	2002–04

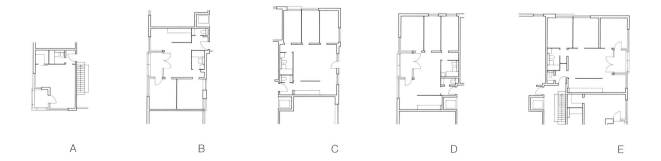

A   B   C   D   E

South facade with loggia
Vertical section
scale 1:20

1 Aluminium sheeting 1 mm
  Plywood panel 40 mm
2 Roof construction:
  Vegetation 80–100 mm
  Protective mat 6 mm
  Separation layer PE membrane
  Polystyrene thermal insulation 120 mm
  Bituminous membrane, double layer
  Reinforced concrete slab 200 mm
3 Pre-cast reinforced concrete element
  with 2° gradient
4 Steel RHS 60 × 40 mm
5 Wall construction:
  Render 20 mm
  Rigid foam thermal insulation 100 mm
  Reinforced concrete 200 mm
6 Insulated glazing in timber casement
7 Floor construction:
  Tufted floor covering 3 mm
  Concrete screed 47 mm
  Separation layer PE membrane
  Sound insulation 25 mm
  Thermal insulation 45 mm
  (ground floor 65 mm)
  Reinforced concrete slab 200 mm
8 Footpath paver 300 × 300 × 40 mm
  Gravel bed 40 mm
  Separation layer
  Polystyrene thermal insulation 100 mm
  Bituminous membrane, double layer
  Reinforced concrete slab 160 mm
9 Aluminium sheeting 1 mm
10 Galvanized steel gutter
11 Artificial (cast) stone 200 × 200 × 80 mm
  Gravel bed

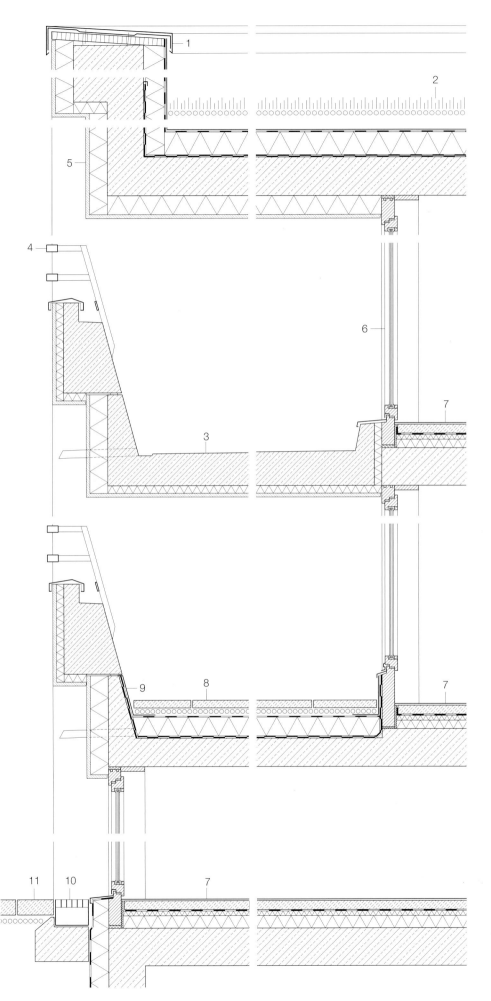

Housing Block in Madrid

Architects: Matos-Castillo Arquitectos, Madrid

This seven storey high social housing development in Madrid contrasts greatly with the typical built fabric of the surrounding environment. The three storey high U-shaped pedestal opens the housing development to the north while supporting three discrete cubic apartment blocks, individually accessed and connected only via the two storey carparking. Breaking down the mass in this way has ensured a lighter impression, in spite of the relatively high density of the complex. The lower floors are provided with natural lighting and fresh air from the light-wells.

The arid climate of Madrid is addressed by the multi-louvred treatment of the facades and the introverted planning. The maisonette dwellings to the east are connected via covered walkways recessed behind precast concrete louvred panels. All other apartments are protected by folding sunscreens with vertical slats inserted in the otherwise architecturally reduced facades of grey panels of varying sizes and materials. The layout of the dwellings is clear and structured, with the kitchens and living areas set back behind loggias.

The longer southern side of the complex accommodates four-room apartments, accessed in pairs from the stairwells – while the squat, square tower of the western side houses three or four smaller dwellings per storey, some of which are orientated inward to the lightwells.

All corridors and apartments of the solid reinforced concrete building are rendered in soft, friendly colours, and the covered walkways, in pastel tones allowing the harsh sunlight to be diffused to a calming, indirect light source.

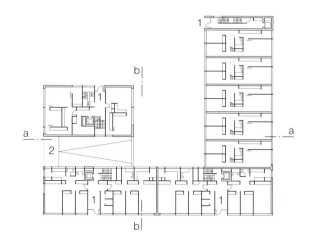

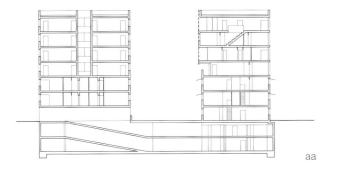

aa

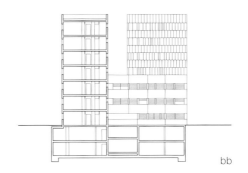

bb

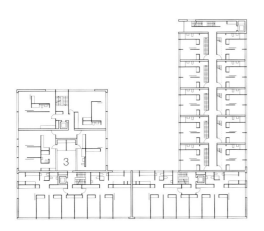

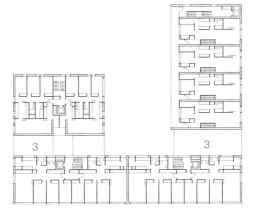

Site plan
scale 1:2000

Floor plans
ground floor,
first and sixth floor
sections
scale 1:750

1 Entrance
2 Driveway to under-
   ground carparking
3 Gallery space

115

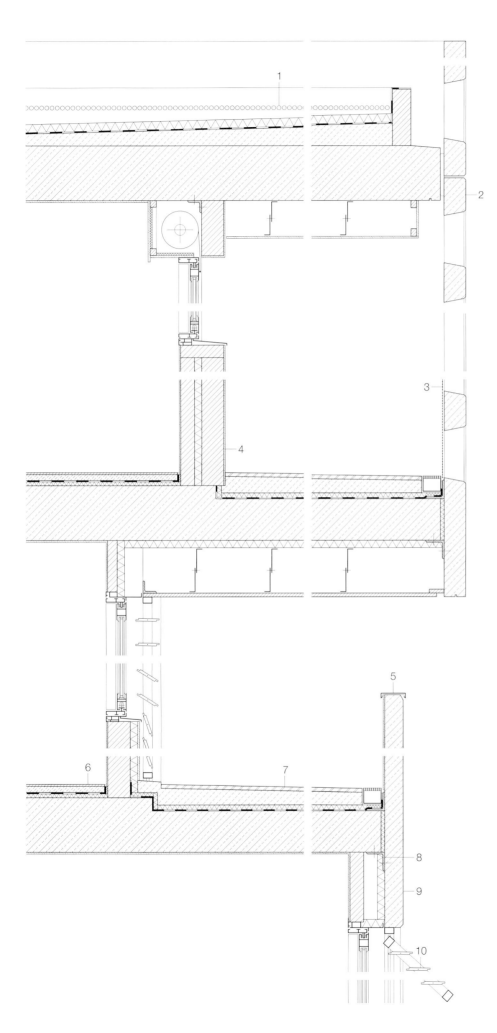

Section of covered walkway
scale 1:20

1 Roof construction:
  Gravel
  Expanded polystyrene thermal
  insulation 50 mm
  Bituminous sheeting, double layer
  Concrete screed
  Reinforced concrete slab 290 mm
  Plasterboard 12.5 mm
2 Precast concrete facade panel 100 mm,
  notched
3 Expanded metal mesh balustrade element
4 Rendered brickwork, double layer
  Polyurethane thermal insulation 40 mm
5 Galvanized steel capping 1.5 mm
6 Oak parquet flooring
7 Terrazzo 20 mm
  Concrete screed 70–90 mm, with gradient
  Expanded polystyrene thermal
  insulation 50 mm
  Bituminous sheeting, double layer
  Reinforced concrete slab 290 mm
  Plaster
8 Steel fixing angle 100 × 100 × 10 mm
9 Precast concrete panel 100 mm
  Polyurethane thermal insulation 40 mm
  Cavity 80 mm
  Rendered brickwork 71 mm
10 Sunscreening with PVC louvres

Project details:
Usage: 68 dwelling units and
                      82 parking spaces in
                      2 underground levels
Units: 5× 1-room apartments
                        (46–50 m²)
                      13× 2-room apartments
                        (54–70 m²)
                      32× 3-room apartments
                        (81–84 m²)
                      18× 4-room maisonettes
                        (89 m²)
Internal room height: 2.60 m
Construction: Reinforced concrete
Unit access: Double unit dwellings
                      and maisonettes with
                      covered walkways
Total floor area: 7,416 m²
Total site area: 3,107 m²
Competition: 2001
Completion: Sep 2003

Apartment Block in Basel

Architects: Morger & Degelo Architects, Basel

The quiet, innercity, landscaped suburb of Gellert in Basel comes to an abrupt end at the intersection with St. Alban-Ring, where the motorway and regional railways have, up until now, disturbed the peace. With the completion of this project by Morger & Degelo; a linear tract protecting the residential location from the noise and pollution of the transport routes in the south, a new, peaceful environment has been created. The triangular building site fronts onto an existing school, with mature planting, and established residences on two sides, only to be confronted with the unavoidable problems of a motorway on the third. The four storey housing block has been utilised here as a noise buffer for the newly created outdoor areas, by being constructed hard on the street frontage and connected directly to existing developments. Polygonal balconies have been used to relieve the rigidity of the long elevation facing the park, and simultaneously to provide as much external living space as possible for the residents. The rhythm of the balconies on the northern side is repeated to the south in a double facade, to provide further sound protection and to make the elevation less formal. Two apartments per storey are connected by each of the four stairwells, which are offset from the party walls, thereby creating larger and smaller dwellings alternatively. Five-room apartments fill the triangular end of the long housing block. All dwellings are orientated north-south requiring the architects to address the problems of location – that the garden side of the complex is to the north, while the south side addresses the traffic. The decision was made, therefore, to provide living spaces oriented in both directions, while the bathrooms and bedrooms divide the layouts into zones. Insitu concrete was used for central core zones, party walls and floor slabs ensuring the requisite shear strength, and all internal walls were constructed of brickwork.

Site plan   scale 1:2000

Project details:
Usage:	45 dwelling units and 11 multi-purpose rooms
Units:	5× 2-room apartments (69.7–79.6 m²)
	16× 3-room apartments (96.9 m²)
	20× 4-room apartments (110.6–118.9 m²)
	4× 5-room apartments (135.2 m²)
Internal room height:	2.51 m
Construction:	Reinforced concrete
Unit access:	Double unit dwellings
Total floor area:	5,688.69 m²
Total site area:	4,577.50 m²
Construction time:	Jan 2001 – Mai 2002

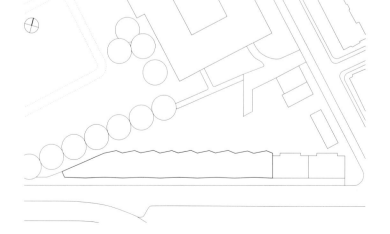

Floor plans
scale 1:750

Housing Blocks in Ingolstadt

Architects: Beyer + Dier, Ingolstadt

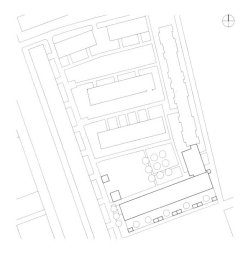

Site plan   scale 1:2500
Floor plans
ground floor, first floor
scale 1:500

The renewal of the southern German city of Ingolstadt included, as one of the largest developments, the revival of the old railway quarter originating from the 1920s. This consisted of an area of three-storey street-frontage apartments which had previously been enhanced by the addition of new balconies. In order to improve the urban landscape and social environment for these inhabitants, while simultaneously providing living spaces for young families, new three storey housing blocks were built on an unused internal communal garden site.

The requisite carparking was provided by renting spaces in a neighbouring high-rise car park. The southern street frontage of the site was closed with a south orientated building connecting directly to an existing building to the east.

A glazed entry hall and central stairway provide access to all 30 apartments via covered walkways. The individual entries are recessed back from the walkways, additional communication zones being thereby created for pairs of dwellings and simultaneously reducing the required access zones within the dwellings.

The solid reinforced concrete construction is clad with grey cement-fibre panels, while the south facing bedroom elevations are clad with thermally insulated, exposed concrete prefabricated sandwich panels. These panels being highly legible on the southern facade.

In order to enhance and personalise the entry zones for the apartments, the internal walls here were clad in laminated timber panels. The warm surface material accentuating the transition from public to private zone. The balustrading panels of the loggias and balconies are constructed of cement-bonded particle board panels colour-coated in pale yellow on both sides.

Project details:
Usage: 30 dwelling units
Units: 26× 2-room apartments
                    (50–54 m²)
                    2× 3-room apartments
                    (70 m²)
                    2× 4-room apartments
                    (85–95 m²)
Internal room height: 2.45 m
Construction: Reinforced concrete
Unit access: Covered walkway
                    accessed apartments
Total floor area: 3,395 m²
Construction time: 2002–04

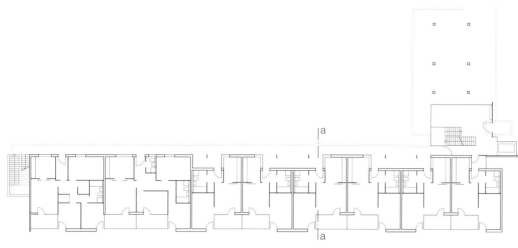

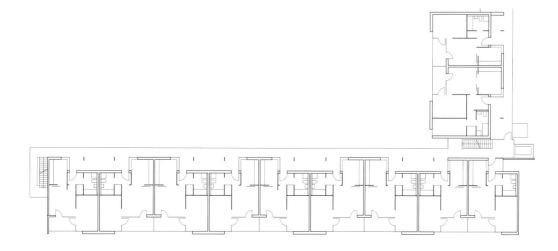

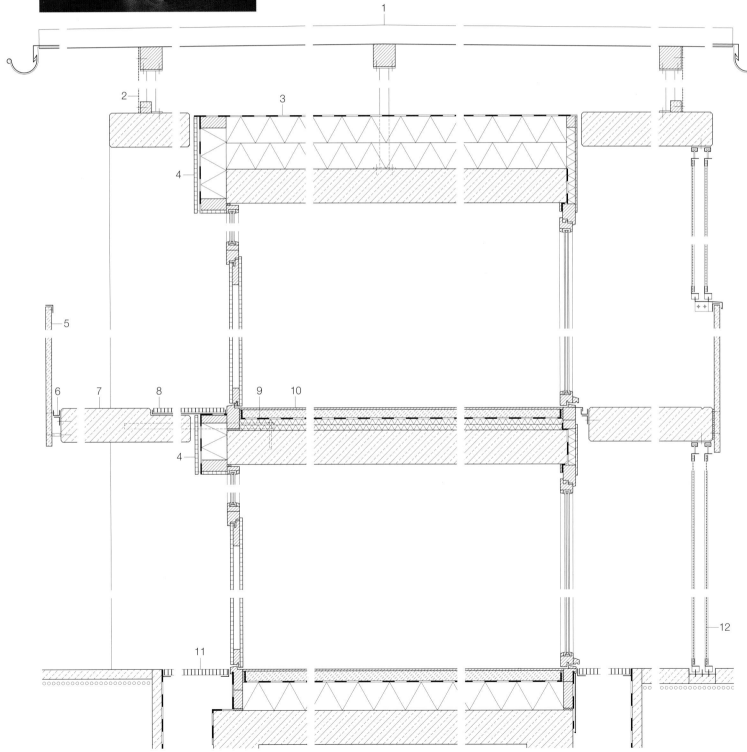

Sections
scale 1:20 · scale 1:500

1 Steel roof sheeting
 Softwood purlin 120 × 120 mm
 Steel RHS standard 50 × 50 × 4 mm
 Cavity
2 Expanded metal insect mesh
3 Diffusion membrane
 Fabric coated mineral wool
 thermal insulation 140 mm
 Mineral wool thermal insulation 140 mm
 Reinforced concrete slab 180 mm, painted
4 Reconstituted timber panel 16 mm
 Batten 20 mm
 Wind-proof barrier
 Fabric coated mineral wool
 thermal insulation 140 mm between
 timber stud construction

5 Balustrading: cement-bonded particle
 board 32 mm, painted yellow
 Steel cover angle 40 × 40 × 4 mm
6 Steel channel 50 × 38 mm
7 Precast reinforced steel element 180 mm
8 Steel grid panel
9 Steel fin 150 × 1000 × 40 mm on
 sound insulating layer
10 Floor construction:
 Oak parquet flooring 10 mm
 Concrete screed 50 mm
 Separation layer
 Sound insulating layer 30 mm
 Thermal insulation 30 mm
 Reinforced concrete slab 180 mm, painted
11 Steel grid panel over light well
12 Expanded metal mesh sliding shutter
 in flat steel framing 30 × 5 mm,
 and steel angle 40 × 40 × 4 mm

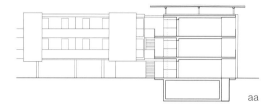

aa

Housing Blocks in Potsdam

Architects: Becher + Rottkamp, Berlin

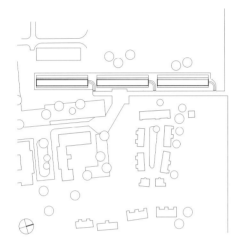

Site plan   scale 1:5000
Floor plans
Standard floor and roof level
scale 1:400

Project details:
Usage:	96 dwelling units
Construction:	Reinforced concrete
Floor areas:	27× 2-room (52–63 m²)
	39× 3-room (78–80 m²)
	22× 4-room (84–93 m²)
	8× 5-room (104 m²) m²
Internal room height:	2.45 m
Unit access:	Double unit access dwellings
Total floor area:	8,850 m²
Residential area:	7,530 m²
Construction time:	2000–02

These three north-south orientated linear blocks accommodating 96 dwellings in Pappelallee in inner-city Potsdam were built as part of a government test-case low-cost housing programme to provide dwellings for public servants. Purist design and an appropriately economical use of materials combine well to produce an attractive environment. The west-facing facades with bands of balconies and storey-high elements of alternating glass and fibre-cement panels, contrast with the punctuated massive facades on the eastern and shorter transverse facades. Four stairwells, each reaching four storeys, are the vertical access routes for each block.

The dwellings, set out in pairs, in four different layouts per storey; are either two, three, or four room apartments and all receive natural lighting from at least two directions. The southern apartments, with openings to, in fact, three sides, are reflected in the central axis of the building, thereby a exciting play of light with the open and closed facade elements.

The recessed roof apartments have more modest floor plans than their lower floor neighbours compensated, however, by the enlarged outdoor areas which extend over the entire widths of the dwellings. The elevated ground floor apartments are designed with terraces and private garden areas, while the upper storey dwellings include deep balconies. The balconies are of water-impermeable, lightweight precast concrete, negating the need for additional paving surfaces. Steel-framed matt-glass dividers between the balconies lend further lightness to the horizontally articulated facades.

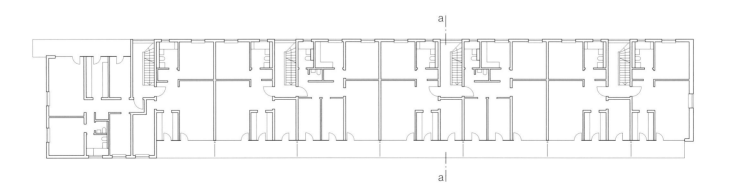

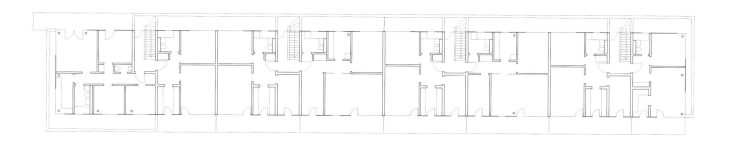

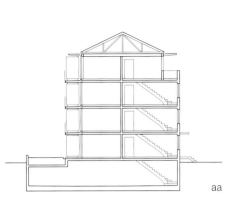

aa

Section   scale 1:400
Section   scale 1:20

 1 Ø 42 mm steel rod handrail galvanized
 2 Ø 38 mm post
 3 Ø 14 mm rod
 4 Ø 20 mm lower chord
 5 ⊔ 160 mm steel channel
 6 120/120 mm steel plate with M 12 threading
 7 drainage gutter (with waterspout)
 8 precast lightweight concrete waterproof
 9 Ø 100 mm downpipe
10 insulated reinforced fixing element
11 floor construction:
    10 mm oak parquet flooring
    60 mm cement screed
    separating layer,
    polythene sheeting
    impact-sound insulation
    40 mm mineral wool
    200 mm reinforced concrete
    Render
12 matt laminated glass divider in steel frame
13 Steel I-beam 160 mm, fireproof encased
    in 15 mm cement-bonded sheeting
14 Roof construction:
    Steel roof sheeting 0.75 mm
    Timber battens 30 × 50 mm
    Timber sandwiched roof construction
    Thermal insulation 160 mm
    Timber battens 40 mm
    Plasterboard, double layer
15 Metal grating, mesh 30 × 30 mm
16 Flat steel fin, welded
17 Steel channel section 180 mm

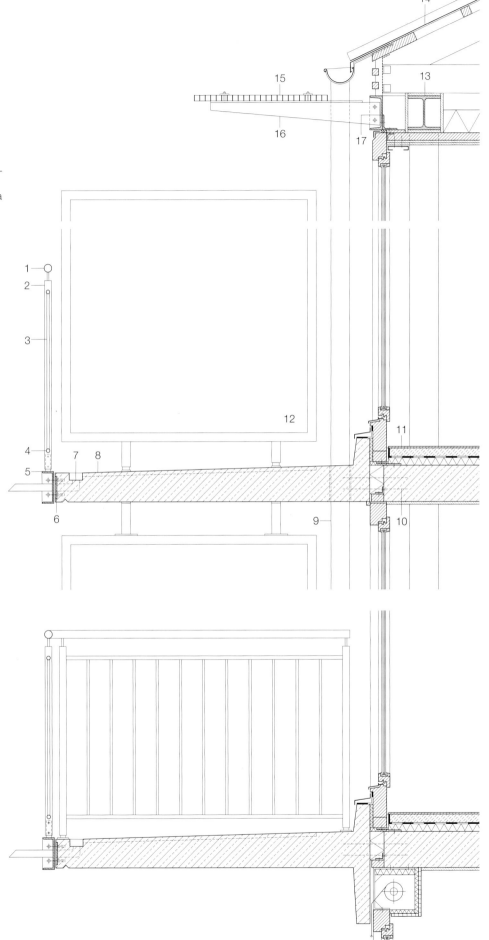

Housing Development in Ingolstadt

Architect: meck architekten, Munich

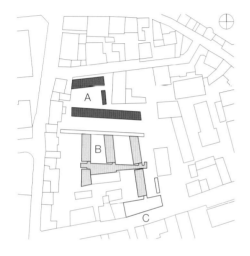

Site plan
scale 1:3000

A First building stage, social housing
B Second building stage, integrated living
C Third building stage, student housing

Second building stage
Section · Elevation
scale 1:250

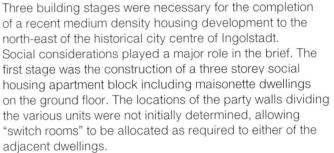

Three building stages were necessary for the completion of a recent medium density housing development to the north-east of the historical city centre of Ingolstadt. Social considerations played a major role in the brief. The first stage was the construction of a three storey social housing apartment block including maisonette dwellings on the ground floor. The locations of the party walls dividing the various units were not initially determined, allowing "switch rooms" to be allocated as required to either of the adjacent dwellings.

The interior planning of the site included a community plaza and meandering paths, accessing the buildings of the second building stage. A concept of integrated living was implemented here, for different social groups; including the elderly, disabled persons, single parents and large families. The planning had to be flexible and avoid the creation of barriers.

A broad central access route on every floor forms the spine of the development and provides ample scope for communication. Adjoining these zones are community spaces, terraced areas, covered access balconies and a lift for disabled persons which ensures a direct link with all dwellings and the basement carparking. The narrow east-west oriented apartments enable less mobile residents to experience the daylight cycle from sunrise to sunset. The dwelling layouts are sub-divided by lightweight partition walling, which can easily be adjusted to accommodate future changes in usage. The access balconies to the east, each serving no more than two apartments, can also be used as outdoor seating areas. The west facade is clad in light grey cement fibreboard. Visual screening for the ceiling height windows is provided by sliding larch shutters which can be controlled by cranking handles located within the apartments.

The third building stage consisted of an apartment building containing 24 dwellings for students, which completed the development at its southern boundary. The ground floor units were again arranged in a maisonette fashion, creating private retreat zones. The apartments on the second and third levels were connected via a double storey recreation area, while the units on the top floor receive indirect north light through sloping roof windows.

At street level, one can easily interpret the internal organisation of the layout. The building is constructed of in-situ concrete; to financial considerations, thermal insulation was limited to the living areas, leaving the projecting recreational zone uninsulated.

aa

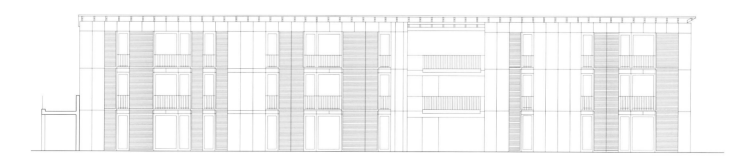

2nd and 3rd buildig stage
Ground floor plan
scale 1:500

Second and third building stages
1 Type 1: 2-room apartment for elderly
2 Type 2: apartment for disabled
3 Type 3: 1½-room apartment
4 Type 4: 3-room apartment for family
5 Community room
6 Adjoining development
7 Double storey access zone
8 Students apartments

Usage types
scale 1:250

A Retreat
B Living
C Communication
D Public zone

Project details, integrated living:
Usage: 33 dwelling units,
                    community space and
                    carparking
Units: 14× 2-room apartments
                        (61 m²)
                    16× 1½-room apartments
                        (50 m²)
                     3× 3-room apartments
                        (75 m²)
Internal room height: 2.44 m
Construction: Massiv brickwork
Unit access: Covered walkway
                    apartments
Total floor area: 4,560 m²
Total site area: 3,400 m²
Construction time: Oct 1995 – Aug 1997

Project details, student housing:
Usage: 24 student apartments
Floor areas: 6× maisonettes
                        (23.6 m²)
                    9× apartments
                        (17.89 m²)
                    9× apartments with
                        gallery (18.31 m²)
Internal room height: 2.43 m (standard)
Construction: In-situ concrete with
                    thermally insulated
                    composite system
Unit access: Covered walkway
                    apartments
Total floor area: 908.29 m²
Total site area: 393 m²
Construction time: Jun 1998 – Aug 1999

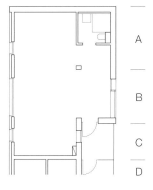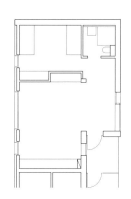

A

B

C

D

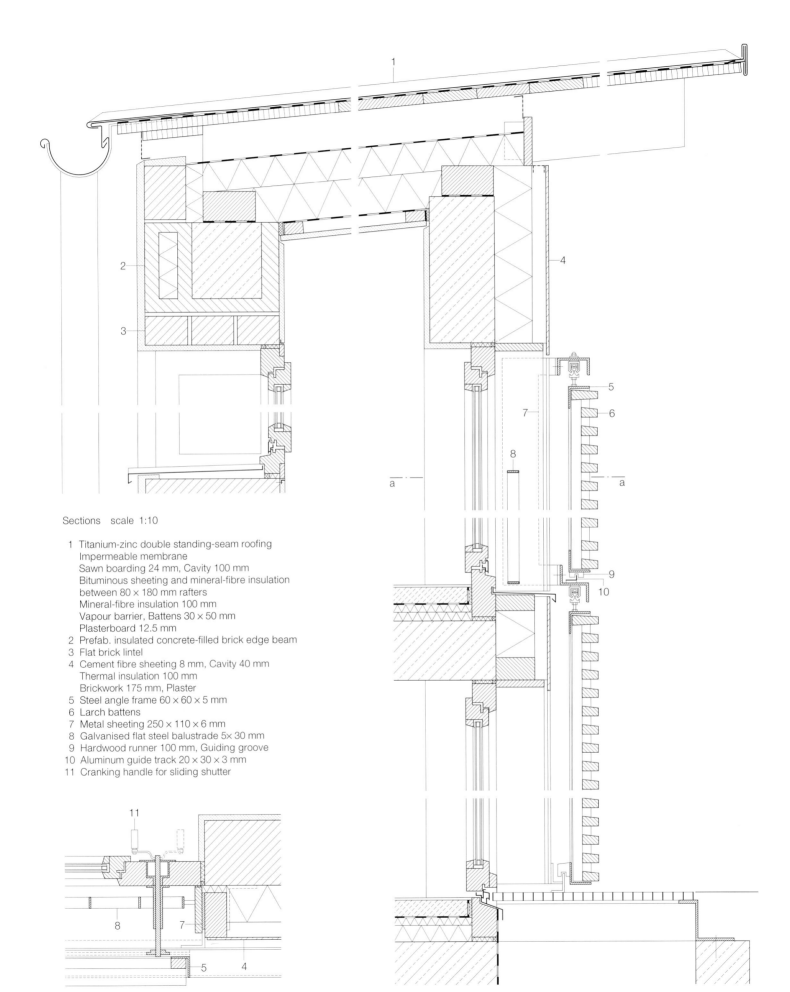

Sections   scale 1:10

1 Titanium-zinc double standing-seam roofing
  Impermeable membrane
  Sawn boarding 24 mm, Cavity 100 mm
  Bituminous sheeting and mineral-fibre insulation
  between 80 × 180 mm rafters
  Mineral-fibre insulation 100 mm
  Vapour barrier, Battens 30 × 50 mm
  Plasterboard 12.5 mm
2 Prefab. insulated concrete-filled brick edge beam
3 Flat brick lintel
4 Cement fibre sheeting 8 mm, Cavity 40 mm
  Thermal insulation 100 mm
  Brickwork 175 mm, Plaster
5 Steel angle frame 60 × 60 × 5 mm
6 Larch battens
7 Metal sheeting 250 × 110 × 6 mm
8 Galvanised flat steel balustrade 5× 30 mm
9 Hardwood runner 100 mm, Guiding groove
10 Aluminum guide track 20 × 30 × 3 mm
11 Cranking handle for sliding shutter

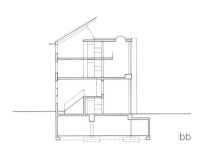

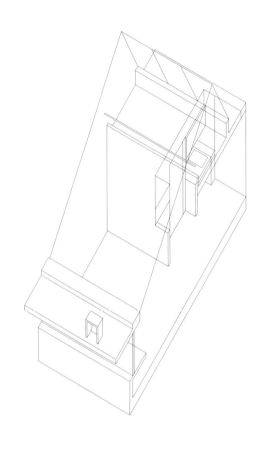

Section   scale 1:500
Axonometric roof apartment
Axonometric maisonette
not to scale

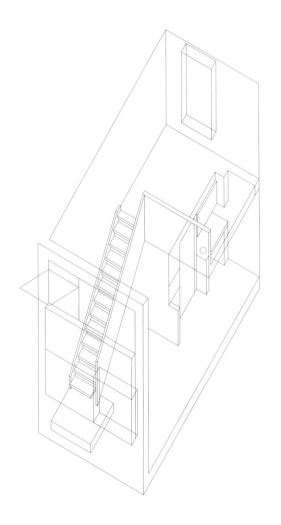

Housing Development in Hanover

Architects: Fink + Jocher, Munich

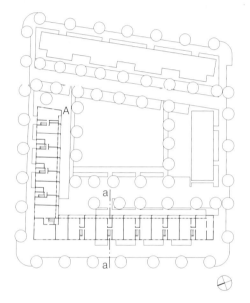

Project details:
Usage: 87 dwelling units, retail space and communal facilities
Construction: Reinforced concrete
Floor areas: 45.4–92.2 m²
Internal room height: 2.46 m
Unit access: Double unit access dwellings
Total floor area: 9,417 m²
Residential area: 6,109 m²
Construction time: 1998–99

Ground floor   scale 1:2000
Floor plan types   scale 1:500

This development of 87 apartments, communal facilities and retail space provided the foundation stone for the new estate of Kronsberg in Hanover. The two predominant elevations of the building relate differently to their environment; the public oriented facade is a product of face klinker brickwork and room-high french windows with traditional folding shutters – while the private, site-internalised elevation is a timber facade recessed behind continuous, deep loggias. The rhythmic, yet slightly off-set, window elements of fixed unit size, lend the street-frontages of the block an interesting plasticity – while simultaneously creating a clear and vibrant image. Single flight stairs connect the dwellings in pairs over five storeys, while the corner stairwell connects three apartments per storey.

A great variety of dwellings has been achieved, ranging from multi-room layouts with central halls to single-room lofts. The structural system of the building is based predominantly upon the load-bearing party walls. The prefabrication of the entire reinforced concrete load-bearing system enabled the construction costs to be greatly reduced. The construction time was reduced to a mere 11 months.

An external face brickwork skin of 115 mm is fixed over 120 mm of thermal insulation which, in turn, is fixed to the reinforced concrete. The parapet is clad with solid precast concrete panels. Window sills and lintels are similarly of precast concrete. The lintels are clad with stretcher bond brickwork, allowing them, upon completion, to have the same surface and depth as the 240 mm deep window reveals. The laminated timber folding window shutters are recessed into the reveals. The facades facing the courtyard are clad in phenolic resin coated birch plywood panels; the loggias create a spatial transition zone to the landscaped courtyard, which stands in great contrast to the surrounding city environment.

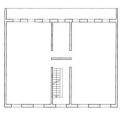

Basic layout

Hall layout

Through-living   Multi-room layout   Island layout   Loft

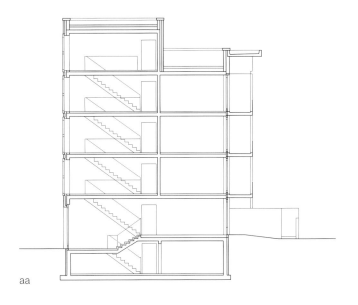

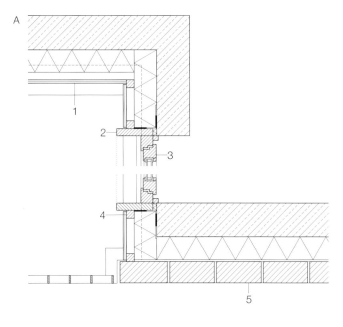

aa

Section   scale 1:250
Horizontal section through junction between
face brickwork and timber panel facade
Horizontal section through apartment window
Horizontal section through stairwell window
Section through street facade
scale 1:20

1 Plywood panel, 18 mm birch, both sides
   coated with phenolic resin
2 Timber reveal 200 × 40 mm
3 Timber framed, with double glazing
4 Supporting construction,
   40 × 40 mm timber sections
5 Wall construction:
   peat-fired facing bricks, NF 115 mm,
   10 mm air space, thermal insulation,
   120 mm mineral fibre
   180 mm reinforced concrete panel
6 4-part folding shutters of 3-ply timber
   boarding, with edge beading in weatherproof
   glue, guide tracks top and bottom,
   2× 15 mm
7 Balustrade of steel flats, galvanized,
   micaceous iron oxide coating, 35 × 8 mm
8 Window sill, precast concrete, overhang with
   drip, 50 mm
9 Timber window, 2 casements,
   with double glazing
10 Horizontal-pivot window, with double glazing,
   spandrel pane fixed, inner pane of laminated
   safety glass
11 Plasterboard 12.5 mm
12 Thermal insulation 80 mm
13 Ring beam, autoclaved aerated concrete
   channel block
14 Rendering 25 mm
15 Terrace construction: pavers in gravel bed,
   15 mm impact sound insulation, waterproofing, 200 mm thermal insulation, vapour
   barrier, 220 mm reinforced concrete slab
16 Sheet metal flashing
17 Parapet/spandrel panel: peat-burned facing
   bricks in stretcher bond, NF 115 mm,
   10 mm air space, thermal insulation, 120 mm
   mineral fibre, 175 mm aerated concrete
18 Open perpend
19 Thermal insulation, 60 mm rigid foam
20 Horizontal groove, with fall to outside
21 Ventilation element
22 Steel angle as support for window sill

138

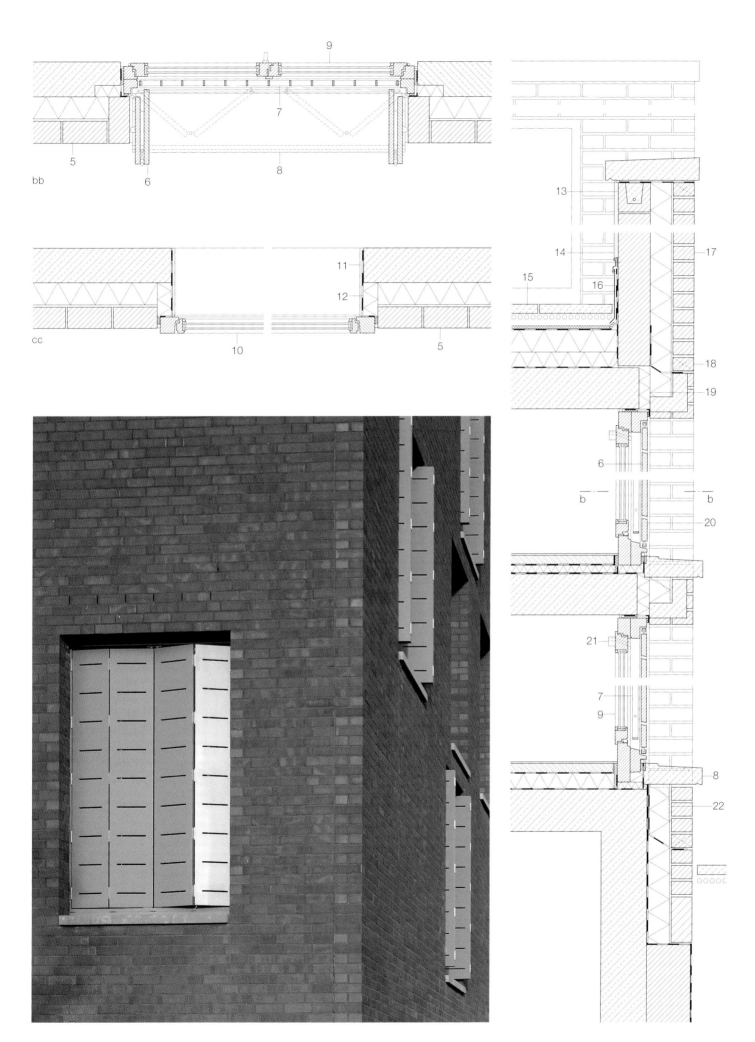

bb

5

6

9

7

8

cc

11

12

10

5

13

14

15

16

17

18

19

6

b   b

20

21

7

9

8

22

139

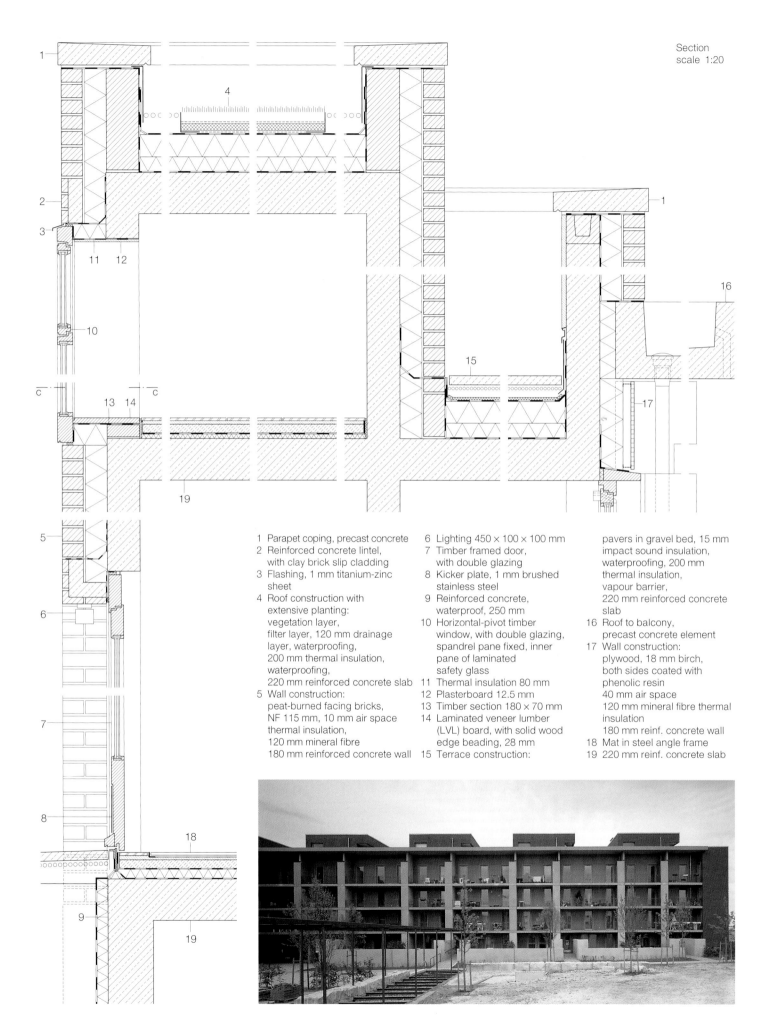

1 Parapet coping, precast concrete
2 Reinforced concrete lintel,
  with clay brick slip cladding
3 Flashing, 1 mm titanium-zinc
  sheet
4 Roof construction with
  extensive planting:
  vegetation layer,
  filter layer, 120 mm drainage
  layer, waterproofing,
  200 mm thermal insulation,
  waterproofing,
  220 mm reinforced concrete slab
5 Wall construction:
  peat-burned facing bricks,
  NF 115 mm, 10 mm air space
  thermal insulation,
  120 mm mineral fibre
  180 mm reinforced concrete wall

6 Lighting 450 × 100 × 100 mm
7 Timber framed door,
  with double glazing
8 Kicker plate, 1 mm brushed
  stainless steel
9 Reinforced concrete,
  waterproof, 250 mm
10 Horizontal-pivot timber
   window, with double glazing,
   spandrel pane fixed, inner
   pane of laminated
   safety glass
11 Thermal insulation 80 mm
12 Plasterboard 12.5 mm
13 Timber section 180 × 70 mm
14 Laminated veneer lumber
   (LVL) board, with solid wood
   edge beading, 28 mm
15 Terrace construction:

pavers in gravel bed, 15 mm
impact sound insulation,
waterproofing, 200 mm
thermal insulation,
vapour barrier,
220 mm reinforced concrete
slab
16 Roof to balcony,
   precast concrete element
17 Wall construction:
   plywood, 18 mm birch,
   both sides coated with
   phenolic resin
   40 mm air space
   120 mm mineral fibre thermal
   insulation
   180 mm reinf. concrete wall
18 Mat in steel angle frame
19 220 mm reinf. concrete slab

Housing Block in Zurich

Architects: Martin Spühler, Zurich

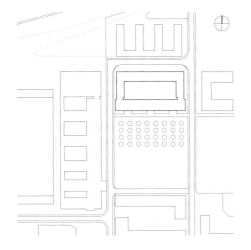

Site plan
scale 1:5000
Section
scale 1:500

This housing development on Oerliker Park, was a part of an urban planning scheme for the renewal of a former industrial area. In order to increase the sunlight entering the central courtyard area, the buildings on the narrow ends of the block were kept to a lower scale than those on the longer sides. The tracts are accessed differently, according to location; the southern building is entered from the central courtyard, the other buildings from the street. Office and retail space is found adjacent to the underground carparking entrance on the ground floors of the end buildings – while all levels of the long side buildings are given over to residential usage. The private outdoor areas connected to the ground floor apartments are either integrated into the general courtyard planning or, when overlooking Oerliker Park, designed as private gardens. The southern tract, adjacent to the park, is subdivided by three full height cavities, which allow a gradation from enclosed courtyard zone to open public park. In this seven storey building, the single storey apartments are accessed by only three stairwells, and take full advantage of the southern facade with full-height glazing, and generously planned entries and private terraces. The six storey building opposite contains both single storey and maisonette dwellings, the character of which is determined by the living-dining areas and the L-shaped loggias. Bedrooms and bathrooms are relegated to the northern facade. The east and west orientated buildings accommodate the smaller apartments, which are also designed inward towards the courtyard, and accessed via covered walkways. The facades overlooking the courtyard and park are generously glazed while the street frontages consist of yellow face brickwork in order to relate to the former built environment.

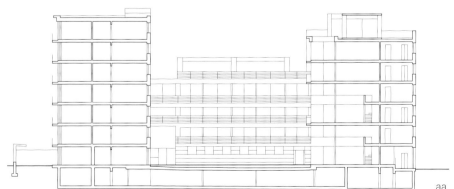

aa

Floor plans
Ground floor
First floor
scale 1:500

1 Maisonette apartment
2 Private outdoor area
3 Courtyard
4 Public entry
5 3½-room apartment
6 Terrace
7 Garden
8 Driveway to underground carparking
9 Retail outlet
10 Office
11 Two storey loggia
12 Balcony
13 2-room apartment
14 Covered walkway

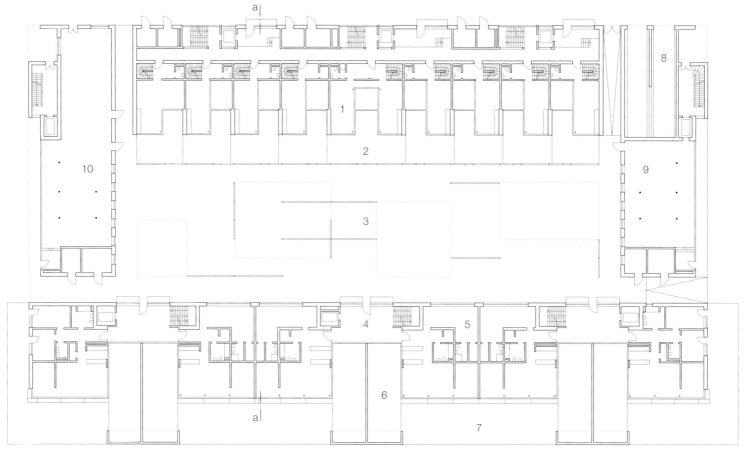

Building Details:
Usage:	106 Dwelling units
Units:	2× 1-room (57 m²)
	4× 1½-room (50 m²)
	8× 2-room (54 m²)
	21× 2½-room (75–85 m²)
	8× 3-room (83 m²)
	7× 3½-room (88–93 m²)
	6× 4-room (110 m²)
	40× 4½-room (115–135 m²)
	6× 5-room (137 m²)
	4× 5½-room (150–157 m²)
Internal room height:	2.40 m
Construction:	Brickwork and reinforced concrete slabs
Unit access:	Covered walkway and multi-unit dwellings
Total floor area:	13,560 m²
Total site area:	6,481 m²
Construction time:	Jul 1999–Oct 2000

1

2

3

4

5

6

7

8

7

8

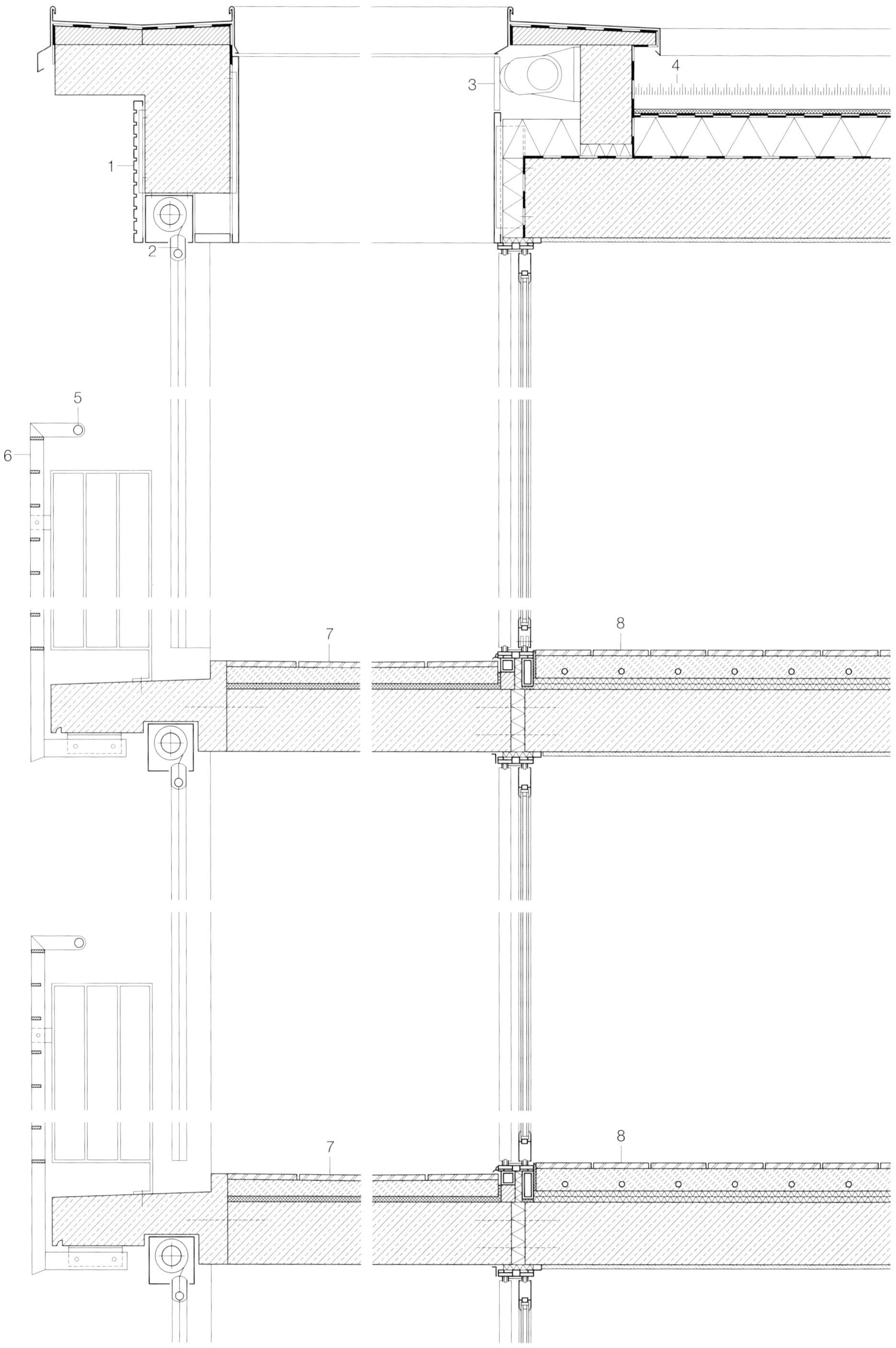

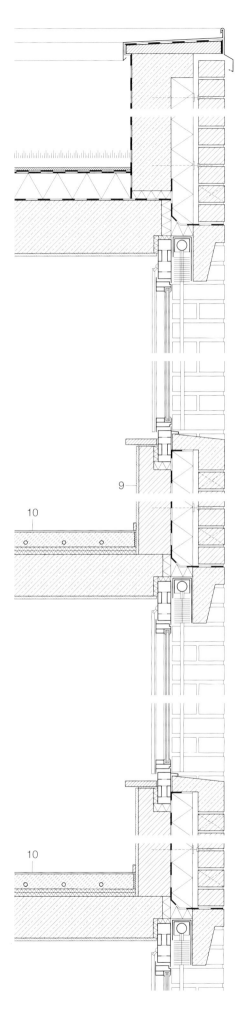

1 Anodized aluminium cladding 500/1.5 mm
2 Fabric sunscreening with guide rail
3 Awning
4 Roof construction:
   Extensive vegetation 50–70 mm
   Rubber granulate protective matting 15 mm
   Polymer-bituminous membrane, double layer
   Foam glass thermal insulation 140 mm
   Vapour barrier bituminous sheeting
   Reinforced concrete slab with
   gradient 240–280 mm
5 stainless-steel tubular handrail diam. 40 mm
6 Galvanized flat steel posts 50 × 12 mm
7 Terrace construction:
   Natural "Porto" slate paving
   in mortar bed 60 mm

liquid plastic coated with sand
8 Floor construction, living area:
   Natural "Porto" slate paving 20 mm
   Concrete screed 80 mm with underfloor heating
   Sound insulation 40 mm, double layer
9 Wall construction:
   Render 15 mm
   Inner leaf brickwork 175 mm
   Mineral wool thermal insulation 120 mm
   Ventilation cavity 30 mm
   Outer leaf face brickwork in
   stretcher bond 140 mm
10 Floor construction, bedroom:
   Linoleum 2 mm
   Concrete screed 80 mm, underfloor heating
   Sound insulation, double layer

147

Housing Development in Munich

Architects: Fink + Jocher, Munich

East of Munich near the village of Riem, bound by motorway, regional railway lines and the new trade fair centre, is a newly developed social housing complex containing 250 dwellings, a kindergarten and high-rise parking.

Three different architectural practices worked in cooperation with each other to develop the area; in order to ensure a unified approach, various constants were determined. The open spaces between the five residential tracts are alternatively green, park area and paved plaza space; access to the various buildings is therefore predetermined by the urban planning. The two rows of apartments designed by Fink + Jocher were in the unusual position of both being accessed from the south. In order to take full advantage of the more attractive south elevations as open space, both internally and externally, it was decided to access the apartments via loggia constructions which were connected directly to the stairwells. The loggias can be rearranged as either open balconies or closed conservatories by sliding glass panels. The dwellings are entered via the loggias through double doors directly into the living area which stretches through to the opposite facade. The kitchen is also orientated to the south, the window looking directly into the stairwell, allowing the residents an uninterrupted view of any visitors at their entrance.

The second floor dwellings are, in fact, maisonettes with roof terraces. The internal stairs are set on the north side above the extra bedrooms of the lower apartments. These bedrooms are located centrally in order to provide an additional room to either of the adjacent dwellings, a so-called "switch room". The red-rendered massive facade addresses the north facing green zone: while the facade to the paved area is composed of extensive glazing and the timber panelled stairwells.

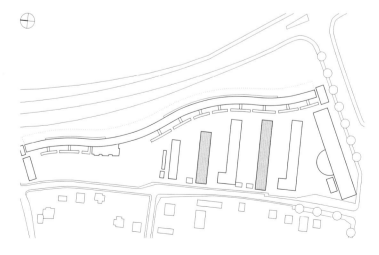

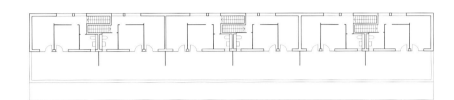

Site plan
scale 1:4000
Floor plans
scale 1:500

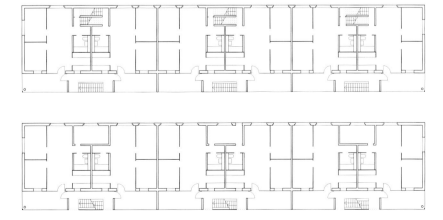

Project details:
Usage: 18 + 24 dwelling units
Units: 14× 3-room apartments
(71 m²)
14× 4-room apartments
(83 m²)
14× 5-room apartments
(107 m²)
Internal room height: 2.425 m
Construction: In-situ brickwork with
reinforced concrete slabs
Unit access: Double unit accessed
dwellings
Total floor area: 2,060 + 2,748 m²
Total site area: Not known
Construction time: Sep 1998 – Jan 2000

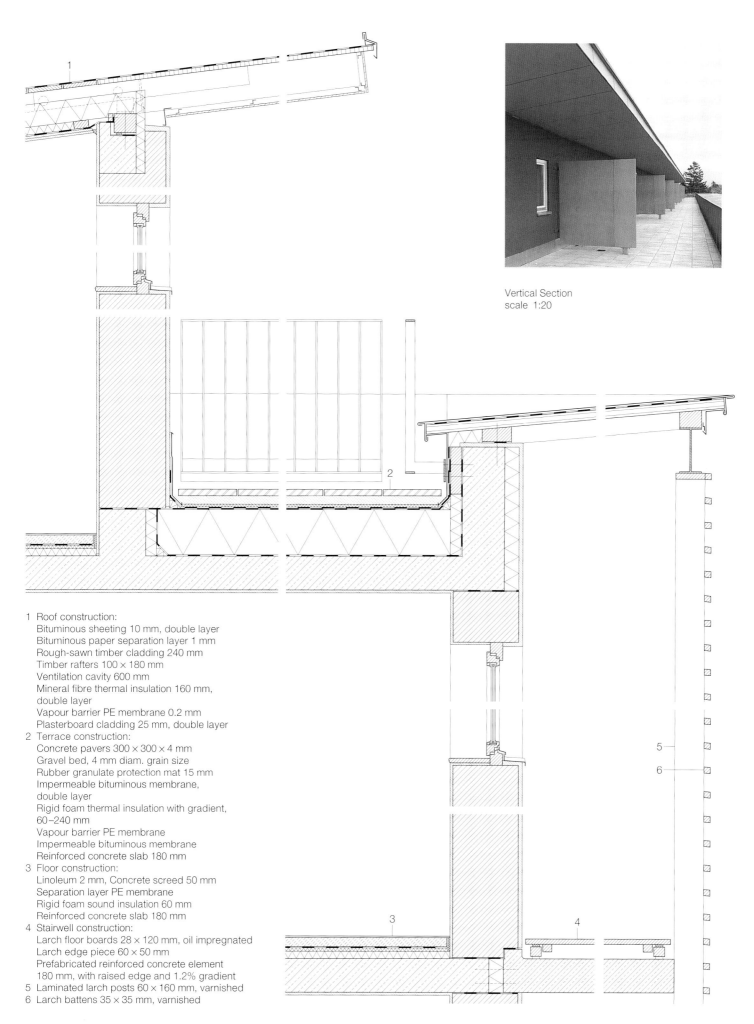

Vertical Section
scale 1:20

1 Roof construction:
Bituminous sheeting 10 mm, double layer
Bituminous paper separation layer 1 mm
Rough-sawn timber cladding 240 mm
Timber rafters 100 × 180 mm
Ventilation cavity 600 mm
Mineral fibre thermal insulation 160 mm,
double layer
Vapour barrier PE membrane 0.2 mm
Plasterboard cladding 25 mm, double layer
2 Terrace construction:
Concrete pavers 300 × 300 × 4 mm
Gravel bed, 4 mm diam. grain size
Rubber granulate protection mat 15 mm
Impermeable bituminous membrane,
double layer
Rigid foam thermal insulation with gradient,
60–240 mm
Vapour barrier PE membrane
Impermeable bituminous membrane
Reinforced concrete slab 180 mm
3 Floor construction:
Linoleum 2 mm, Concrete screed 50 mm
Separation layer PE membrane
Rigid foam sound insulation 60 mm
Reinforced concrete slab 180 mm
4 Stairwell construction:
Larch floor boards 28 × 120 mm, oil impregnated
Larch edge piece 60 × 50 mm
Prefabricated reinforced concrete element
180 mm, with raised edge and 1.2% gradient
5 Laminated larch posts 60 × 160 mm, varnished
6 Larch battens 35 × 35 mm, varnished

Two Housing Blocks in Berlin

Architects: popp.planungen, Berlin

A gaping hole in the built fabric of Prenzlauer Berg in Berlin has been filled with the completion of a development comprising two new housing blocks and the renovation of an existing rear building. Together they provide 33 dwellings and 7 office units. The demographic range of the residents spans from teenagers to the elderly, almost half of which live in familiy units. The first 12 leasable apartments were completed in the initial building stage, the stairwell dividing each of the seven storeys into two apartments. The core zone for kitchens and bathrooms is centrally located, while the living areas stretch the depth of the building and are oriented east-west. A 1.80 m wide elevated zone is located internally adjacent to the facade. The light-colouring of the beech parquet flooring of this "Estrade" elevates it visually above and beyond the comparatively darker blue of the epoxy resin floor surface of the internal spaces. This "Estrade", functioning as a transition zone between the internal rooms and the external balconies can be utilized as bedrooms, living rooms or loggias. In the apartments the kitchen, bathroom and entrance hall are separated from the living area by a ten metre long concertinaed wall; comprising 12 separate timber veneered panels which can be individually rotated or folded together as desired. The second construction stage is of 12 owner-occupied apartments, of 94 m² each. The room dividers in this development, however, are of black varnished timber partition walling in the form of storage units or shelving combinations. The "Estrades" in this building, project partially into the living areas, creating L-shaped zones. With the exception of the liftwells and the basements, all load-bearing walls in both buildings are constructed of 24 cm concrete blockwork, while the prefabricated exposed concrete slabs span up to 9.50 m.

Site plan
scale 1:2500

Floor plan variations
Leasable apartments
Floor plans
scale 1:250

1 Leasable apartments
2 Owner-occupied
  apartments
3 Renovated rear
  building
4 Living area
5 Bathroom
6 WC
7 Storage
8 Kitchen
9 Internal "Estrade"
10 External "Estrade"/
  Balcony

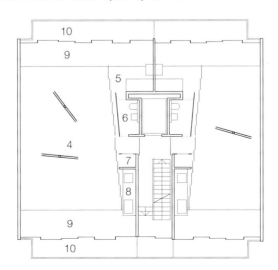

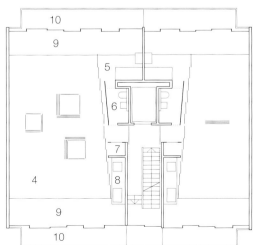

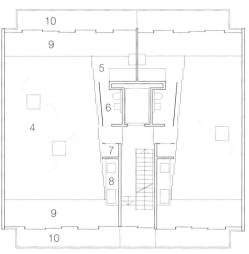

Standard section
Floor plan variations
Owner-occupied apartments

scale 1:250

1 Living area
2 Bathroom
3 WC
4 Entrance hall
5 Kitchen
6 Internal "Estrade"
7 External "Estrade
8 Dressing room

Project details:
Usage:	24 dwellings and 7 office units
Units:	12× leasable apartments (108 m² and 78 m²)
	12× owner-occupied apartments (94 m²)
Internal room height:	2.70 m
Construction:	Sand-lime brickwork with reinforced concrete hollow-core plank slabs
Unit access:	Double unit accessed dwellings
Total floor area:	1,357 + 1,485 m²
Total site area:	829 + 460 m²
Construction time:	Feb. 1996 – Feb. 1998, Jul 2000 – Sept 2001

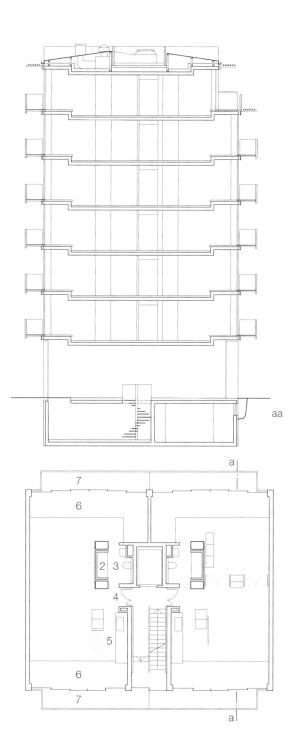

aa

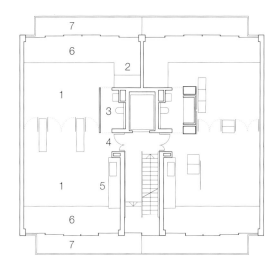

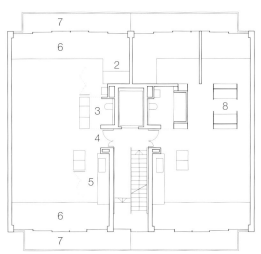
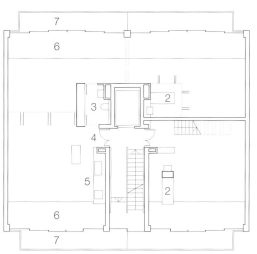

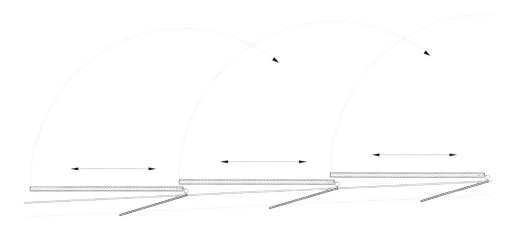

System section
Concertinaed wall   scale 1:20

Alder timber veneer panels 22 × 840 × 2640 mm
on 7 mm flat steel,
painted matt black,
with pivotting hinges.
Sub-construction guides
with pins and channels

Vertical section facade
scale 1:20

1 Sunscreening:
   Larch beams 40 × 80 mm, oiled
   Flat steel 15 × 90 mm, welded to
   Steel I-beam 240 mm
2 Balcony construction:
   Timber decking untreated Bangkirai 25 mm,
   Impermeable PE membrane, multi-layered
   Thermal insulation 100 mm
   Equalising layer "Perlite" 28–58 mm
   Separation layer
   Hollow plank pre-stressed concrete 200 mm
3 Floor construction:
   In-situ epoxy-resin 5 mm,
   Cement screed 50 mm
   Separation layer, Sound insulation 30 mm
   Separation layer
   Hollow plank pre-stressed concrete 200 mm
4 Floor construction "Estrade":
   Solid Beech parquet flooring 28 mm, oiled
   Concrete screed 50 mm, Separation layer
   Sound insulation 30 mm, Separation layer
   Hollow plank pre-stressed concrete 200 mm
5 Flat steel balustrade posts 15 × 90 mm
   Steel rod top chord diam. 66 × 3 mm
   Stainless steel fabric,
   fixings with shroud fixings

158

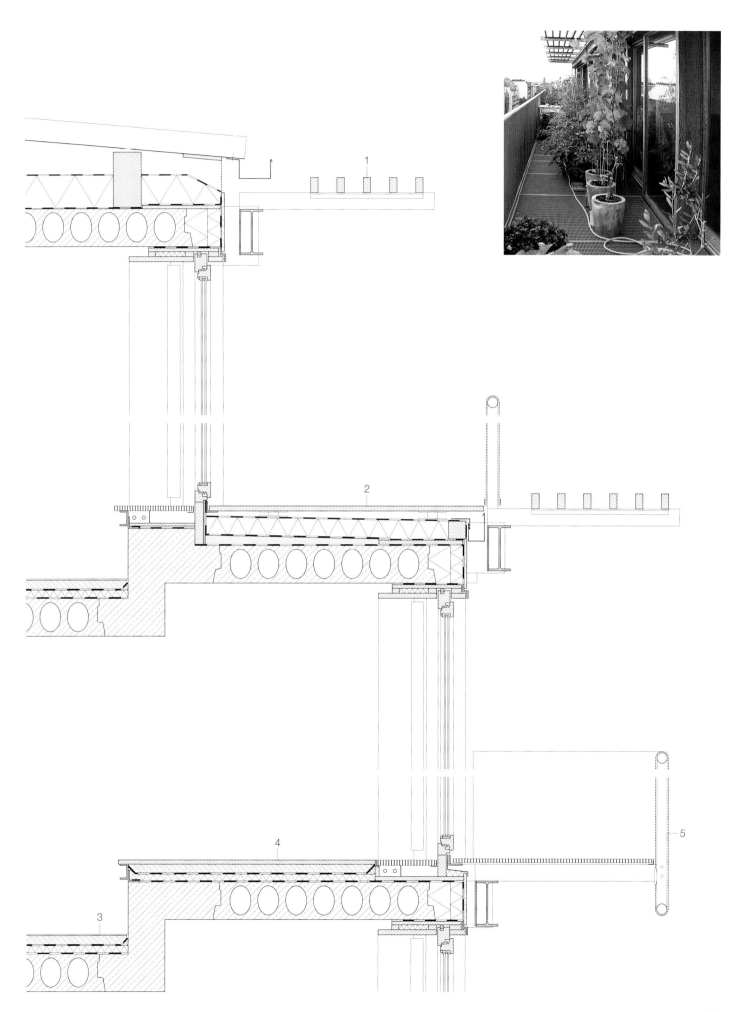

City block in Rotterdam

Architects: KCAP, Rotterdam
Kees Christiaanse, Irma van Oort, Hiltje Huizenga

Project details:

Usage:	458 dwelling units
	112 aged dwellings and
	retail outlets
Units:	Apartments (71–187 m²)
	Aged dwellings
	(80–110 m²)
Internal room height:	2.40 m
Construction:	Reinforced concrete with
	blockwork
Unit access:	Covered walkway,
	multi-dwelling units and
	single access dwellings
Total floor area:	70,000 m²
Total site area:	24,240 m²
Construction time:	1999–2002

Site plan   scale 1:5000

A Single-storey apartments
  balcony above conservatory
B Single-storey apartments
  external corridor above
  conservatories
C Maisonette apartments

KCAP drew up the development plan for a 60,000 m² site in Rotterdam. They planned the buildings at each end of the plot, other architects designed those in between. In total, 600 new apartments were built, 5,000 m² of retail and office space, a junior school and many courtyards. By variously applying a number of constant design elements, KCAP created a wide range of building types, high in quality and perfectly suited to inner-city residential use. The 16 four and eight storey apartment blocks each have a different ground plan and facade design, responding to the different traffic situations, orientation and needs of the residents. Yet an overall visual harmony is maintained as the facades all share the same basic design – engineering-brick facing in various colours and surface textures. This forms the background for a strong, overlaying structure of oriel elements – conservatories or projecting bays with balconies above – positioned more or less closely across the facades. Two of the apartment blocks, designed for older people, are accessed via covered external corridors, conceived as oriel-like features supported from below. One block, close to a busy junction, is almost entirely enclosed in a second skin of conservatories that filter noise and interrupt the cuboid geometry of the eight-storey volume. The buildings on the residential streets within the development are designed like terraced houses and are only four storeys high. Here the oriel element extends over two floors, lighting the single-aspect living room behind, or it appears as an entrance area in front of the typical Dutch-style staircase leading to the apartment in the upper storeys.

The different treatment of a standard oriel element thus gives ample scope for individual arrangement.

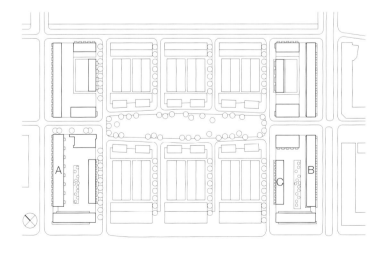

Sections · Standard floor layouts
Scale 1:400

A Single-storey apartments
   balcony above conservatory
B Single-storey apartments
   external corridor above
   conservatories
C Maisonette apartments

1 Oriel/conservatory
2 Balcony
3 External corridor
4 Retail space
5 Access to maisonette on 2nd floor

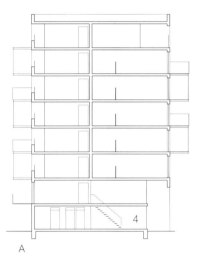

A

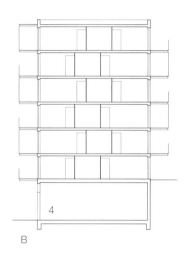

B

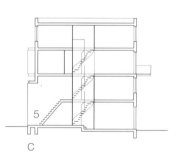

C

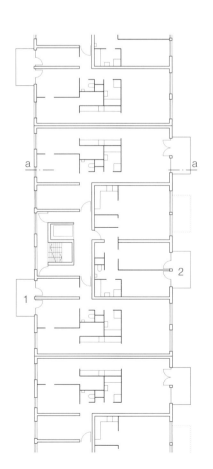

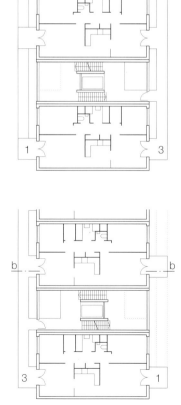

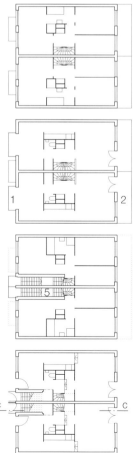

Oriel · Conservatory
Sections scale 1:20

1 steel I-beam, 160 mm deep, thermo-galvanized
2 100 mm face brickwork
   35 mm ventilated cavity
   120 mm mineral-wool thermal insulation
   120 mm sand-lime brickwork
3 8 mm single-glazed sliding window
4 floor construction of balcony or external corridor:
   22 mm wooden boards on firring
   double sealing layer
   18 mm composite timber board
   46/96 mm wrot timber between steel girders
   12 mm composite ceiling board
5 ventilation component
6 steel flat for horizontal bracing

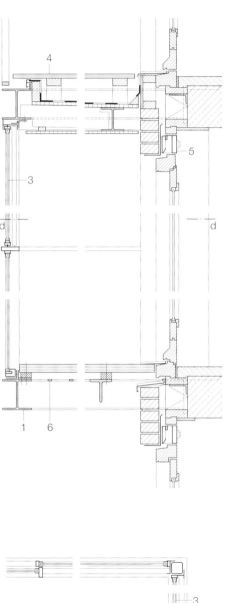

Housing in Ludwigsburg

Architects: Hartwig N. Schneider
in collaboration with Gabriele Mayer, Stuttgart

Site plan   scale 1:2500
Floor plans · Section
Second floor, Ground floor
scale 1:500

Project details:
Usage:	60 dwelling units and
	2 underground car parks
Units:	13× 1-room (38 m²)
	36× 2-room (55–60 m²)
	11× 3-room (72 m²)
Internal room height:	2.42 m
Construction:	Brickwork with reinforced
	concrete slabs
Unit access:	Covered walkway and
	multi-dwelling units
Total floor area:	7,220 m²
Total site area:	3,874 m²
Construction time:	Oct 1995 – Jun 1997

Sixty publicly funded dwellings with underground carparking were realized in this quiet location, nestled between the city centre of Ludwigsburg and its outskirts; surrounded by developments dating from the 1950s. The project continued in the tradition of the open urban planning of the area, while simultaneously achieving a high level of density. A wide range of residents was catered for; singles, couples, single-parent-households and families.

L-shaped blocks were laid out around three half-open courtyards, while an elongated block to the south screens these courtyards from a public park. Accommodated in this longer building are ground floor maisonette appartments, accessible from the north; and upper level single-storey dwellings, reached via covered walkways.

The dwellings arranged around the courtyards, with 1–3 rooms and occasionally extending over two storeys, receive daylight from two or even three sides. Economic yet spacious layouts, which are not immediately legible from the facades, are achieved in two ways – the length of the main living areas extends through the entire depth of the dwellings and the internal walls are set back from the facade.

On the west elevations the loggias to the living rooms are enclosed by sliding window elements. The bedrooms can be darkened by means of glass sliding shutters with enamelled rear surfaces.

The tree-lined courtyards are linked to the street via flights of stairs and to the gardens to the south via covered open areas. Naturally ventilated underground carparking is provided in the plinth storey beneath the courtyards.

Because of the poor load-bearing capacity of the subsoil, 1,100 broken-stone piles were constructed to strengthen the foundations. The outer walls of the buildings are in light-weight brickwork with pigmented mineral render. The wall surfaces react tonally to changes in the weather conditions. In contrast, the south-facing walls overlooking the gardens are clad with pre-fabricated untreated cedar elements with integrated timber sliding shutters and small, pre-coloured, precast concrete balconies. The fenestration consists of timber frames and heat-absorbing glass. In particularly exposed situations, timber and aluminium casements were used.

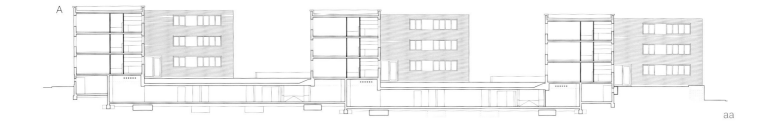

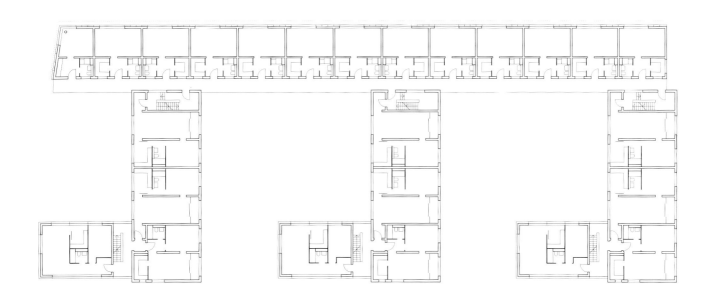

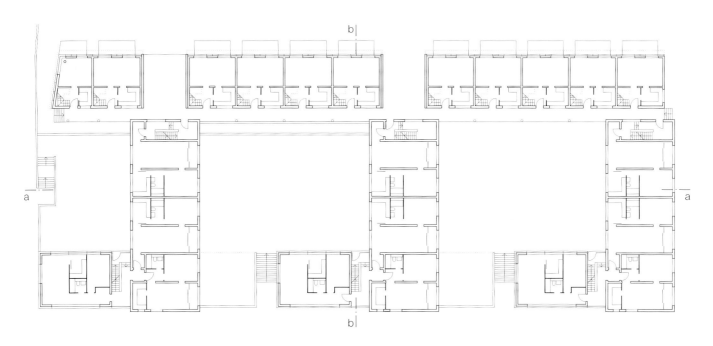

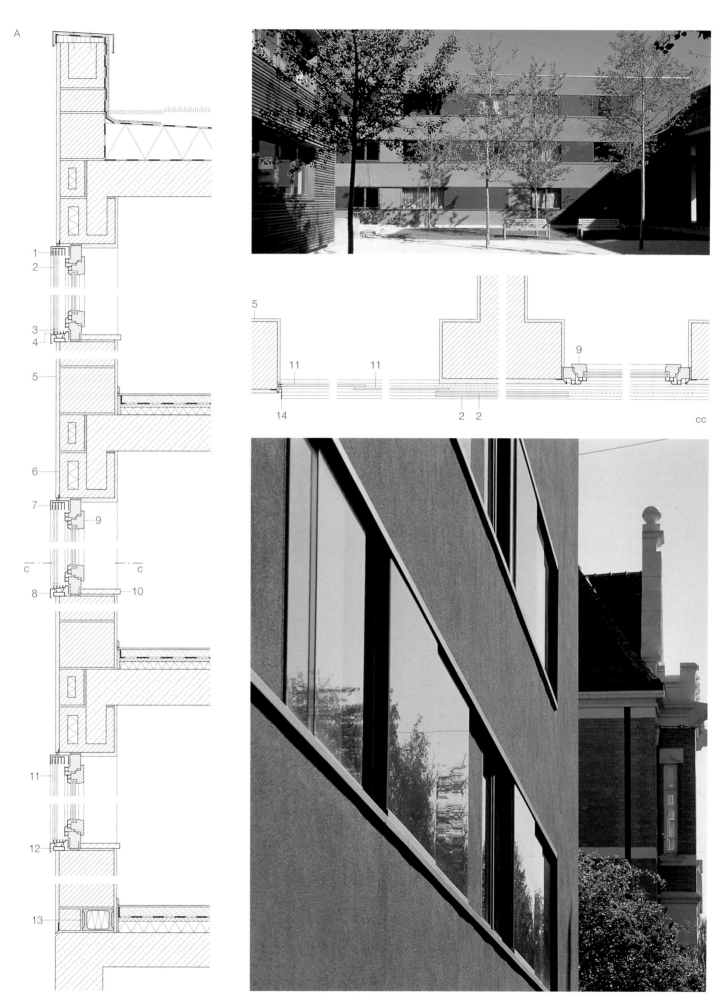

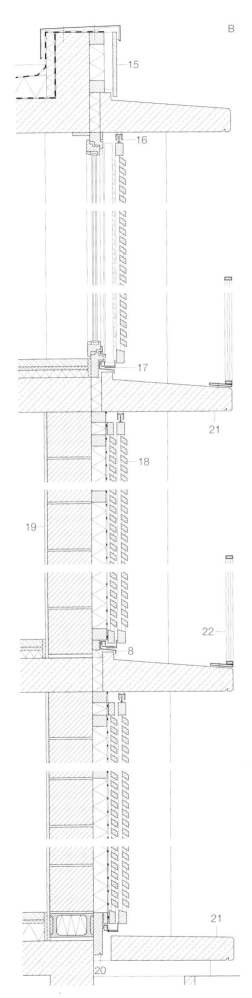

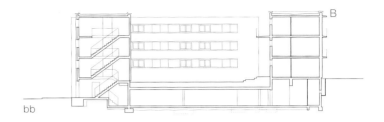

Section through west facade
Horiontal section through sliding glazing in
rendered facade   scale 1:20
Section   scale 1:500
Section through south facade   scale 1:20

1 Aluminium track, with brushes
2 Toughened safety glass, 8 mm,
   rear face enamelled
3 Aluminium guide shoe, with guide wheel
4 Aluminium track
5 Wall construction: 20 mm mineral rendering
   300 mm Hlz lightweight clay bricks
   15 mm internal plaster
6 Lightweight clay channel block, 300 mm
7 Aluminium channel 100 × 50 × 5 mm
8 Aluminium external window sill
9 Wood/aluminium window, double glazing

10 Reconstituted stone internal window sill
11 Toughened safety glass, 8 mm
12 Stainless steel profile
13 Galvanized RHS 60 × 20 × 3 mm
14 Aluminium angle 60 × 30 × 5 mm
15 14 mm cement-bound wood fibre board
16 Upper track for sliding shutters
17 Lower track
18 Cedar wood shutters, 58 mm
19 Wall construction: 15 mm internal plaster
   240 mm Hlz lightweight clay bricks
   80 mm mineral wool thermal insulation
   protective covering (non-woven fabric)
   prefabricated cedar wood cladding, 58 mm
20 Timber closing piece 220 × 48 mm
21 Precast concrete element, coloured
22 Balustrade of steel sections, galvanized,
   colour-coated

Bibliography

Bibliography

Broto, Carles: New Housing Concepts, Gingko Press, Corte Madera 2002

Carduff, Christian; Kuster, Jean-Pierre (eds.): Wegweisend wohnen. Gemeinnütziger Wohnungsbau im Kanton Zürich an der Schwelle zum 21. Jahrhundert, Scheidegger & Spiess, Zurich/Frankfurt 2000

Crosbie, Michael J. (ed.): Multi-Family Housing: The Art of Sharing, Images Publishing Group, Victoria 2003

Dirlmeier, Ulf (ed.): Geschichte des Wohnens Band 2. 500–1800 Hausen, Wohnen, Residieren, Deutsche Verlags-Anstalt, Stuttgart 1998

ETH Wohnforum Zürich, Stadtplanungsamt Bern (ed.): Stand der Dinge. Wohnen in Bern, exhibition catalogue, a supplement to Hochparterre 10/2003

Faller, Peter: Der Wohngrundriss, Deutsche Verlags-Anstalt, Stuttgart/Munich 2002

Flagge, Ingeborg (ed.): Geschichte des Wohnens Band 5. 1945 – heute Aufbau, Neubau, Umbau, Deutsche Verlags-Anstalt, Stuttgart 1999

French, Hilary (ed.): Accomodating in Change: Innovation in Housing, Architecture Foundation, London 2002

Gausa, Manuel: Housing. New Alternatives, New Systems, Birkhäuser Verlag, Basel/Boston/Berlin 1998

Hochbaudepartment der Stadt Zürich, ETH Zürich, Wüest & Partner (ed.): Stand der Dinge. Neuestes Wohnen in Zürich, exhibition catalogue, Zurich 2002

Hoepfner, Wolfram (ed.): Geschichte des Wohnens Band 1. 5000 v. Chr.–500 n. Chr. Vorgeschichte, Frühgeschichte, Antike, Deutsche Verlags-Anstalt, Stuttgart 1999

Isphording, Stephan: Bauen und Wohnen in der Stadt. Stadthäuser, Aufstockungen, Nachverdichtungen, Deutsche Verlags-Anstalt, Stuttgart/München 2003

Kähler, Gert (ed.): Geschichte des Wohnens Band 4. 1918–1945 Reform, Reaktion, Zerstörung, Deutsche Verlags-Anstalt, Stuttgart 1996

Kloos, Maarten; Wendt, Dave (ed.): Formats for Living. Contemporary floor plans in Amsterdam, Arcam, Amsterdam 2000

Landesinstitut für Bauwesen des Landes Nordrhein-Westfalen (ed.): Stadtsiedlungen für die Zukunft. Wohnungen auf Entwicklungsstandorten, Aachen 2000

Lindner, Gerhard; Schmitz-Riol, Erik: Systembauweise im Wohnungsbau, Verlag Bau+Technik, Düsseldorf 2001

Mehlhorn, Dieter-Jürgen: Grundrissatlas Wohnungsbau, Bauwerk Verlag, Berlin 2000

Mostaedi, Arian: Apartment Architecture Now, Gingko Press, Corte Madera 2003

Oberste Bayerische Baubehörde (ed.): Wohnmodelle Bayern – Band 3. Kostengünstiger Wohnungsbau, Callwey Verlag, Munich 1999

Oberste Bayerische Baubehörde (ed.): Wohnmodelle Bayern. Qualität für die Zukunft, Callwey Verlag, Munich 2004

Reulecke, Jürgen (ed.): Geschichte des Wohnens Band 3. 1800–1918 Das bürgerliche Zeitalter, Deutsche Verlags-Anstalt, Stuttgart 1997

Stamm-Teske, Walter (ed.): Preiswerter Wohnungsbau in Österreich, Verlag Bau+Technik, Düsseldorf 2001

Stamm-Teske, Walter (ed.): Preiswerter Wohnungsbau in den Niederlanden, Verlag Bau+Technik, Düsseldorf 1998

Schader-Stiftung (ed.): wohn:wandel. Szenarien, Prognosen, Optionen zur Zukunft des Wohnens, Darmstadt 2001

Schneider, Friederike (ed.): Grundrissatlas Wohnungsbau / Floor Plan Manual: Housing, Birkhäuser Verlag, Basel/Boston/Berlin, 3rd revised and expanded edition, 2004

Tichelmann, Karsten; Pfau, Jochen: Entwicklungswandel Wohnungsbau. Neue Gebäudekonzepte in Trocken- und Leichtbauweise, Vieweg Verlag, Braunschweig/Wiesbaden 2000

Waechter-Böhm, Liesbeth (Hrsg.): Carlo Baumschlager & Dietmar Eberle. Über Wohnbau / Houseing, Springer-Verlag, Vienna/New York 2000

Wicky, Gaston; Selden, Brigitte: Neues Wohnen in der Schweiz. Architekten und Bauten im Porträt, Deutsche Verlags-Anstalt, Stuttgart/Munich 2003

Wüstenrot Stiftung (ed.): Wohnbauen in Deutschland, Karl Krämer Verlag, Stuttgart/Zurich 2002

Journals

archithese, 4/2003 Wohnbauprogramme / Programmes d'habitation

arquitectura+tecnología, 1/2002 densidad / density I

arquitectura+tecnología, 2/2002 densidad / density II

arquitectura+tecnología, 1/2003 densidad / density III

arquitectura+tecnología, 2/2003 densidad / density IV

Baumeister, 7/2003 Bauen für den Wohnungsmarkt

Detail, 3/2003 Konzept Wohnungsbau / Housing

Deutsche Bauzeitung, 8/2002 Wohnen auf der Etage

werk, bauen + wohnen, 6/2001 Wohnen, wohnen / Habitats / Housing

werk, bauen + wohnen, 10/2002 Stadtvillen, Stadthäuser, Parkhäuser

Authors

Christian Schittich (editor)

Born in 1956
Studied architecture at the Technical University, Munich,
followed by seven years of practical experience in the field; publicist;
since 1991 member of the editorial team at DETAIL, since 1992 co-editor;
since 1998 editor in chief;
author and editor of numerous books and journal articles.

Klaus-Dieter Weiß

Born in 1951
Author and publicist, lives in Minden/Westphalia.
Studies in Munich and Aachen, research and teaching positions at the Institute
for Design and Architecture, Technical University Hanover;
correspondent for "architektur.aktuell" und "werk, bauen + wohnen".
Numerous essays and books on various themes in modern and contemporary
architecture.
Since 1981, publications on housing typology.

Eberhard Wurst

Born in 1960
Study of architecture and urban planning,
from 1992–98 scientific collaboration in the Peter Faller's research
project "Der Wohngrundriss"; independent architecture practice since 1992;
since 1998 research, publications and lectures on housing, building science and
urban planning, lectureship at the Fachhochschule Konstanz in 2002;
since 2003 lectureship at Stuttgart University.

Project details/Architects

Housing Developement in Zurich

Client:
FGZ Familienheim-Genossenschaft, Zurich
Architects: ARGE
EM2N Architekten ETH/SIA
Mathias Müller, Daniel Niggli, Zurich; bosshard + partner
Baurealisation
AG, Zurich
Project management: Christof Zollinger
Associates: Marc Holle, Wolfgang Kessler, Christoph Rothenhöfer
ct Bauökonomie AG, Zurich
Structural engineering for solid construction:
Tragwerk GmbH, Affoltern a. Albis
Structural engineering for timber construction: ARGE
Pirmin Jung Ingenieure für Holzbau, Rain; Makiol + Wiederkehr Holzbauingenieure HTL/SISH, Beinwil am See
Landscape architects:
Zulauf Seippel Schweingruber, Baden

em2n@em2n.ch
http://www.em2n.ch

Mathias Müller
Born in 1966; 1996 diploma at ETH (Swiss Federal Institute of Technology), Zurich;
since 1997/98 office partnership EM2N Architekten ETH/SIA.

Daniel Niggli
Born in 1970; 1996 diploma at ETH, Zurich; since 1997/98 office partnership EM2N Architekten ETH/SIA.

Housing Block in Merano

Client:
Baugesellschaft Wolkenstein, Meran Architects:
Holzbox Tirol, Innsbruck
Anton Höss, Innsbruck
Structural engineering:
Vorarlberger Ökohaus, Ludesch
Erich Huster, Bregenz

mailbox@holzbox.at
www.holzbox.at

Erich Strolz
Born in 1959; 1980–1989 studies in Graz and Innsbruck; since 1993 office partnership with Armin Kathan in Innsbruck.

Armin Kathan
Born in 1961; 1981–1998 studies in Vienna and Innsbruck; since 1993 office partnership with Erich Strolz in Innsbruck.

Housing Development in Dornbirn

Client:
I+R Schertler GmbH, Lauterach
Architects:
B & E Baumschlager-Eberle, Lochau
Project management:
Harald Nasahl
I+R Schertler GmbH, Lauterach
Associate:
Christine Falkner
Structural engineering:
Rüsch, Diem, Schuler and Eric Hämmerle, Dornbirn
Landscape architects:
Vogt Landschaftsarchitekten, Zurich

office@baumschlager-eberle.com
www.baumschlager-eberle.com

Carlo Baumschlager
Born in 1956; since 1985 office partnership with Dietmar Eberle; teaching since 1994.

Dietmar Eberle
Born in 1952; since 1985 office partnership with Carlo Baumschlager; teaching since 1983; since 1999 professor at the ETH, Zurich.

Housing Development in Trofaiach

Client:
GIWOG – Gemeinnützige Industrie-Wohnungsaktiengesellschaft, Leonding
Architect:
Hubert Riess, Graz
Associate:
Christoph Platzer
Supervision:
WAG Linz, Christian Schmied
Structural engineering:
Rudolf Prein, Loeben

Architekt.riess@aon.at

Hubert Riess
Born in 1946; 1967–1975 studies in architecture at the Technical University (TU) Graz; 1976–1977 assistant at the TU Graz; since 1985 self-employed architect in Graz; 1992 visiting professor at the TU Munich; 1994 professor at the Bauhaus University, Weimar.

Housing Towers in Constance

Client:
Bauherrengemeinschaft Bismarcksteig, Constance
Architects:
Ingo Bucher-Beholz, Gaienhofen
Associates:
Andy Brühlmann, Jo Zanger, Tom Klettner
Structural engineering:
Ingenieurbüro Olaf Leisering, Constance
General contractor:
Friedrich Wieland GmbH & Co. KG Singen

Ingo Bucher-Beholz
Born in 1959; 1980–1985 studies at Biberach College (Fachhochschule, FH); 1990–1993 independent architecture studio in Constance; 1993–1994 teaching at the Biberach College; 1999–2002 lectureship at Constance College; since 1993 independent architecture office.

Residential and Commercial Centre near Copenhagen

Client:
TK Development A/S, Danton A/S
Architects:
Arkitektfirmaet C. F. Møller, Copenhagen
Associates:
Anna Maria Indrio, Jørgen Juul
Søren Aagaard, Charlotte Hyldahl
Christian Hanak, Mette Hofmann-Bertelsen
Structural engineering:
Søren B. Nielsen Aps, Naestved
General contractor:
Danton A/S, Randers

www.cfmoller.com
kbh@cfmoller.com

Anna Maria Indrio
Born in 1943; 1965–1970 studies at the Royal Academy of Art, Copenhagen; since 1991 partner at Arkitektfirmaet C. F. Møller.

Housing in Tokyo

Client:
The Urban Development
Corporation Architects:
Riken Yamamoto & Field Shop,
Yokohama structural engineering:
Takumi Orimoto Structural Engineer
& Associates + Urban Develop-
ment Corporation +
JV of Mitsui Sumitomo, Konoike +
Dai Nippon Construction
General contractor:
JV of Mitsui Sumitomo, Konoike,
and Dai Nippon Construction

field-shop@riken-yamamoto.co.jp
www.riken-yamamoto.co.jp/

Riken Yamamoto
Born in 1945; 1968 B.A. at Nihon
University; 1971 M.A. at Tokyo
National University of Fine Arts and
Music; since 1973 independent
architecture firm Riken Yamamoto
& Field Shop.

Housing Blocks in Gifu, Japan

Client:
Gifu Prefecture
Architects:
Kazuyo Sejima and Associates,
Tokyo
Local architect:
Yamasei Sekkei, Gifu
Structural planning:
O.R.S. Office, Tokyo
Main contractor 1st stage:
Usami-Gumi, Gifu
Main contractor 2nd stage:
Tsuchiya-Gumi, Gifu

Kazuyo Sejima
Born in 1956; 1981 diploma at
Japan's Women University;
1987 founded the Kazuyo Sejima &
Associates, Tokyo architectural

practice; 1995 founded SANAA
with Ryue Nishizawa; since 2000
visiting professor at the ETH,
Zurich; currently professor at
Keio University.

Patio Houses in Amsterdam

Client:
Bouwbedrijf m.j.de Nijs
en Zonen bv
Architects:
MAP Arquitectos,
Josep Lluís Mateo, Barcelona
Structural engineering:
Ingenieursgroep van Rossun,
Almere

map@mateo-maparchitect.com
www.mateo-maparchitect.com

Josep Lluís Mateo
Born in 1949; 1973 diploma at the
"Escuela Téchnica Superior de
Arquitectura" (ETSAB or School of
Architecture), Barcelona; 1976
teaching at the ETSAB; 1991
founded MAP Arquitectos
architecture practice in Barcelona;
1994 doctorate at ETSAB; since
1994 professor at ETSAB; visiting
professor at several universities,
among others at UP8 (Paris 1987),
OAF Oslo Arkitektforening (Oslo
1990) and at the ETH, Zurich
(1993–1995).

Housing Development in Paris

Client:
Régie Immobilière de la Ville
de Paris
Architects:
Herzog & de Meuron, Basel

Project team:
Andrea Bernhard, Béla Berec
(model), Christine Binswanger,
Jacques Herzog, Robert Hösl,
Sacha Marchal, Mario Meier
(structural consultant),
Pierre de Meuron
Construction supervision:
Cabinet A. S. Mizrahi, Paris
General contractor:
Bouygues SA, Paris

info@herzogdemeuron.ch

Jacques Herzog
Born in 1950; 1975 diploma in
architecture at the ETH, Zurich; in
1978 established firm with Pierre de
Meuron; since 1999 professor at
the ETH Studio Basel; since 2002
professor at the ETH Studio Basel,
Institute for the Contemporary City.

Pierre de Meuron
Born in 1950; 1975 diploma in
architecture at the ETH, Zurich; in
1978 established firm with Jacques
Herzog; since 1999 professor at
the ETH Studio Basel; since 2002
professor at the ETH Studio Basel,
Institute for the Contemporary City.

Housing Block in Munich

Client:
Bauland GmbH München
Architects:
meck architekten, Munich
Associates:
Peter Fretschner, Peter Sarger,
Wolfgang Amann
Structural engineering:
Ingenieurbüro
Haushofer Tragwerk & Plan GmbH,
Markt Schwaben

office@meck-architekten.de
http://www.meck-architekten.de

Andreas Meck
Born in 1959; 1985 diploma at the
TU Munich; DAAD scholarship
Architectural Association London,
graduate diploma 1987; since 1989
independent office in Munich; since
1998 professor of Design and
Construction at the FH Munich;
since 2001 meck architekten.

Two Housing Blocks in Munich

Client:
Heimag München
ZF Generalbau München
Architects:
Rohnke Hild und K
Munich: Andreas Hild, Dionys
Ottl, Tilmann Rohnke
Associates:
Nina Grosshauser
Structural engineering:
Stegerer and Zuber, Munich

Architekten@hildundk.de
www.Hildundk.de

Andreas Hild
Born in 1961; 1988 diploma at TU
Munich; since 1998 Hild und K
Architekten in partnership with
Dionys Ottl; since 2001 project
partnerships with Tilmann Rohnke;
2003–2004 visiting professor at the
HfbK (University of Fine Arts),
Hamburg.

Dionys Ottl
Born in 1964; 1995 diploma at TU
Munich; since 1999 partner at
Hild und K; since 2001 project
partnerships with Tilmann Rohnke.

Tilmann Rohnke
Born in 1961; 1986 diploma at ETH,
Zurich; since 1992 independent
architectural practice in Munich;
since 2001 project partnerships
with Hild und K.

Housing Block in Madrid

Client:
Empresa Municipal de la Vivienda
Ayuntamiento de Madrid
Architects:
Matos-Castillo Arquitectos, Madrid
Structural engineering:
Valladares Ingenieros, Madrid
Building contractor:
IMASATEC.S.A, Madrid

matos-castillo@infonegocio.com

Alberto Martínez Castillo
Born in 1960; since 1985 office
partnership with Beatriz
Matos Castaño; since 1987
professor at the E.T.S. of Architecture in Madrid.

Beatriz Matos Castaño
Born in 1954; since 1985 office
partnership with Alberto Martínez
Castillo; since 1989 professor at the
E.T.S. of Architecture and at the
European University C.E.E.S in
Madrid.

Apartment Block in Basel

Client:
Anlagestiftung Pensimo Manage-
ment AG Zürich
Architects:
Morger & Degelo Architekten BSA
SIA, Basel
Meinrad Morger, Heinrich Degelo,
Benjamin Theiler
Associates:
Dagmar Strasser, André Buess
General contractor:
Mobag AG, Allschwill

mail@morger-degelo.ch

Meinrad Morger
Born in 1957; study of architecture
at HTL Winterthur; since 1988 office
partnership with Heinrich Degelo;
guest lecturer at the EPFL,
Lausanne and at the ETH, Zurich;
since 2003 lecturer at the School of
Technology and Architecture in
Lucerne.

Heinrich Degelo
Born in 1957; study of interior
decoration and product design at
the School of Design, Basel;
collaboration with the architecture
firm Herzog & de Meuron, Basel;
since 1988 office partnership with
Meinrad Morger.

Benjamin Theiler
Born in 1970; study of architecture
at the ETH, Zurich; since 2002
partner at Morger & Degelo.

Housing Blocks in Ingolstadt

Client:
Gemeinnützige Wohnungsbau-
Gesellschaft Ingolstadt GmbH
Architects:
Beyer +Dier, Ingolstadt
Associates:
Rosmarie Probeck
Structural engineering:
Grad Ingenieurplanungen,
Ingolstadt

info@beyer-dier.de

Franz Beyer
Born in 1961; 1981–1986 study of
architecture at the FH Munich;
1986–1989 planning office for
building construction; 1989–1991
independent architecture practice;
since 1991 office partnership with
Detlef Dier.

Detlef Dier
Born in 1961; 1983–1989 study of
architecture at the FH Munich;
since 1991 office partnership with
Franz Beyer; 1990–1994 lecturer at
the FH Munich; since 1995 lecturer
at the TU Stuttgart.

Housing Blocks in Potsdam

Client:
Deutschbau Immobilien-
Dienstleistungen GmbH
Architects:
Becher + Rottkamp, Berlin
Associates:
Horst Schönig (project manager/
planning), Patrick Roos (project
manager/execution)
Structural engineering:
HEG Beratende Ingenieure, Berlin
Landscape planning:
Heiner Wortmann, Lüdinghausen
General contractor:
Wiemer & Trachte AG, Potsdam

mail@becher-rottkamp.de
www.becher-rottkamp.de

Andreas Becher
Born in 1960; 1988 degree at the
University-GH, Paderborn;
1989–1991 Fulbright Scholarship at
the Virginia Polytechnic Institute
Blacksburg, USA; 1993 founded
Becher +Rottkamp Architekten.

Elmar Rottkamp
Born in 1963; 1987 degree at the
University-GH, Paderborn;
1988–1990 Dortmund University;
1993 founded Becher + Rottkamp
Architekten.

Housing Development in Ingolstadt

Client:
Gemeinnützige Wohnungsbau-
Gesellschaft GmbH, Ingolstadt
Architects:
meck architekten, Munich
Execution planning and building
supervision: in collaboration with
Klaus Greilich
(2nd building phase) and Stephan
Köppel

(3rd building phase), Munich
Associates (2nd building phase):
Matthias Goetz, Michaela Busen-
kell, Christoph Engler,
Brigitte Moser
Project management (3rd building
phase):
Werner Schad
Associates (3rd building phase):
Susanne Frank
Structural engineering:
Ingenieurbüro Schittig, Ingolstadt

office@meck-architekten.de
www.meck-architekten.de

Andreas Meck
Born in 1959; 1985 diploma at TU
Munich; DAAD scholarship at the
Architectural Association London,
with graduate diploma in 1987;
since 1989 independent practice
in Munich; since 1998 professor
of Design and Construction at
FH Munich; since 2001 meck
architekten.

Housing Development in Hanover

Client:
Gesellschaft für Bauen und
Wohnen mbH, Hanover
Architects:
Fink + Jocher, Munich
Associates:
Ivan Grafl (project manager),
Rüdiger Krisch, Ulrike Wietzorrek
Landscape architects:
Landschaftsarchitektur Diekmann,
Hanover
General contractor:
Phillip Holzmann AG, Hanover

architekten@fink-jocher.de
www.fink-jocher.de

Dietrich Fink
Born in 1958; 1984 diploma at TU
Munich; 1987–1988 founded
architecture practice with Karlheiz
Brombeiß and Nikolaus Harder;
since 1991 office partnership with
Thomas Jocher; since 1999
professor at TU Berlin.

Thomas Jocher
Born in 1952 in Benediktbeuren;
1980 diploma at TU Munich; since
1991 office partnership with
Dietrich Fink; since 1997 professor
at the University of Stuttgart.

Housing Block in Zurich

Client:
Credit Suisse
Real Estate Management, Zurich
Architects:
Martin Spühler, Zurich
General contractor:
Batigroup AG, Zurich
Structural engineering:
Proplaning AG, Basel

www.spuehler.ch
spuehler@spuehler.ch

Martin Spühler
Born in 1942; 1963–1967 study of
architecture at the Academy of Fine
Arts, Vienna; 1967 diploma, state
examination, master examination
award; since 1978 independent
architecture practice in Zurich.

Housing Development in Munich

Client:
GEWOFAG Munich
Architects:
Fink + Jocher, Munich
Associates:
Markus Dobmeier (project
manager), Silvia Braun,
Uli Kostka, Erika Mühlthaler,
Christian Ruhdorfer
Landscape architects:
Berger + Reitsam, Freising
Structural engineering:
Ingenieurbüro Hingerl, Munich

architekten@fink-jocher.de
www.fink-jocher.de

Dietrich Fink
Born in 1958; 1984 diploma at
TU Munich; 1987–1988 founded
architecture practice with Karlheiz
Brombeiß and Nikolaus Harder;
since 1991 office partnership with

Thomas Jocher; since 1999
professor at TU Berlin.

Thomas Jocher
Born in 1952 in Benediktbeuren;
1980 diploma at TU Munich;
since 1991 office partnership with
Dietrich Fink; since 1997 professor
at the University of Stuttgart.

Two Housing Blocks in Berlin

Client:
Wolfram Popp, Berlin
Architects:
popp.planungen, Berlin
Associates:
Gregor Siber
Structural engineering:
Johann Schneider, Berlin

popp@popp-planungen.de
www.popp-planungen.de

Wolfram Popp
Born in 1957; self-taught, formally
recognized as graduate engineer
at the TU Stuttgart; 1984–1986 film
architect; 1991–1994 study of
philosophy at the Freie Universität,
Berlin; 1996 lecturer at the Bauhaus
University, Weimar; since 1994
office popp.planungen, Berlin;
currently visiting professor at the
TU Berlin.

City block in Rotterdam

Client:
Stadstuinen CV, Estrade Wonen,
Leyten & Partners, Woonzorg
Architects:
KCAP, Rotterdam
Kees Christiaanse, Irma van Oort,
Hiltje Huizenga
Structural engineering:
Ingenieurs bureau Zonneveld b.v,
Rotterdam

post@kcap.nl
www.kcap.nl

Kees Christiaanse
Born in 1953; 1988 diploma at TU
Delft; since 1996 professor at TU
Berlin; since 1989 independent
architecture practice in Rotterdam:
Kees Christiaanse Architects &
Planners KCAP; 1990 founded
ASTOC, Cologne; since 2003
professor at the ETH, Zurich.

Irma van Oort
Born in 1965; 1991 diploma at
TU Delft; since 1992 associate at
KCAP, from 1998 onward as
director and partner.

Ruurd Gietema
Born in 1964; 2002 diploma at
TU Delft; since 1996 associate at
KCAP; since 2002 partner at KCAP.

Han van den Born
Born in 1958; 1987 diploma at
TU Delft; since 1998 associate at
KCAP; since 2002 director and
partner at KCAP.

Housing in Ludwigsburg

Client:
Wohnungsbau Ludwigsburg
GmbH, Ludwigsburg
Architects:
Hartwig N. Schneider in
collaboration with Gabriele Mayer,
Stuttgart
Project architects:
Andreas Gabriel, Ingo Pelchen
Associates:
Franz Lutz
Structural engineer:
Hans-Walter Jäger, Ludwigsburg

info@hartwigschneider.de
www.hartwigschneider.de

Hartwig N. Schneider
Born in 1957; 1977–1984 study of
architecture at the University of
Stuttgart and at the Illinois Institute
of Technology in Chicago, USA;
1990 established own architecture
firm, collaboration with Gabriele
Schneider; 1991–1994 lectureship
at the University of Stuttgart; 1998
professor at TU Berlin; since 1999
professor at the University of
Technology (RWTH), Aachen.

Illustration credits

The authors and editor wish to extend their sincere thanks to all those who helped to realize this book by making illustrations available. All drawings contained in this volume have been specially prepared in-house. Photos without credits are from the architects' own archives or the archives of "DETAIL, Review of Architecture". Despite intense efforts, it was not possible to identify the copyright owners of certain photos and illustrations. Their rights remain unaffected, however, and we request them to contact us.

from photographers, photo archives and image agencies:

- Autorengruppe Wohnungsbau: Hertelt, Raith, van Gool, Karlsruhe: p. 29
- Blee, Sarah, Antwerp: p. 39
- Dittmann & Dittmann, Ebenhausen: pp. 129, 131, 133
- Fabijanic, Damir, Zagreb: pp. 62–64, 66–67
- Frederiksen, Jens, Copenhagen: pp. 76–77
- Halbe, Roland/artur, Cologne: pp. 164, 167
- Henz, Hannes, Zurich: pp. 47–48, 51–53
- Heinrich, Michael, Munich: pp. 105–108, 110–112, 134–135
- Hueber, Eduard, New York: pp. 10, 37, 58–59, 61
- Hoch, Giorgio, Zurich: pp. 142–145, 147
- Horn, Peter C., Stuttgart: pp. 148–149
- Hurnaus, Hertha, Vienna: p. 41
- Kaltenbach, Frank, Munich: p. 163
- Kandzia, Christian, Stuttgart: p. 166
- Kasper, Guido, Constance: pp. 71–72, 74–75
- Kiwitt, Stephanie, Leipzig: p. 34
- Malagamba, Duccio, Barcelona: pp. 86–88, 95
- Meyer, Stefan, Berlin: pp. 155, 156 top, 158
- Müller, Stefan, Berlin: pp. 125, 127
- Ohashi, Tomio, Tokyo: pp. 78–79
- Roth, Lukas, Cologne: pp. 137–141
- Scagliola, Daria, Rotterdam: p. 92
- Schicker, Christa, Munich: p. 150
- Schittich, Christian, Munich: pp. 8, 26, 60, 109, 113
- Schneider, Uwe Lukas, Munich: pp. 120–123
- Schuster, Oliver, Stuttgart: p. 35
- Shinkenchiku-sha, Tokyo: pp. 81–85
- Simon, Isabel, Berlin: p. 157
- Spiluttini, Margherita, Vienna: pp. 96–103
- Suzuki, Hisao, Barcelona: pp. 114–117
- 't Hart, Rob, Rotterdam: pp. 42, 162
- Tessaro, Manuela, Bozen: pp. 54–57
- van der Vlugt, Ger, Amsterdam: p. 93
- Vile, Philip/Haworth Tompkins, London: p. 11
- Walti, Ruedi, Basel: pp. 118–119

from books and journals:

- Benevolo, Leonardo: Die Geschichte der Stadt, Frankfurt 1983, p. 932: p. 18 bottom
- Hartmann, Monika, Koblin, Wolfram: selber + gemeinsam planen, bauen, wohnen, Munich 1978, p. 42: p. 22
- Highrise of Homes. SITE, New York 1982, p. 56/57: p. 12; p. 42: p. 23
- Klotz, Heinz (Hrsg.), Vision der Moderne, Munich, 1986, p. 351: p. 21
- Le Corbusier: La Ville radieuse, Paris, 1964, p. 292: p. 18 top, p. 247: p. 19
- Peichl, Gustav: Wiener Akademie-Reihe (Hrsg.). Wiener Wohnbau Beispiele, Wien 1985, p. 58: p. 20
- Ragon, Michel: Wo bleiben wir morgen?, Munich 1963, p. 93: p. 25
- Schader-Stiftung (Hrsg.): wohn:wandel. Szenarien, Prognosen, Optionen zur Zukunft des Wohnens, Darmstadt 2001, p. 280: p. 28
- Schulze-Fielitz, Eckhard; Stadtsysteme I, Stuttgart 1971, p. 58: p. 24

Articles and introductory b/w photos:

p. 8; Women's dormitory in Kumamoto, Kumaoto Prefecture, Japan, Kazuyo Sejima and Associates, Tokyo
p. 12; Highrise of Homes; SITE, New York
p. 26; Housing Development in Innsbruck; Georg Driendl, Vienna

Dust-jacket photo:
Housing Block in Zurich
Architects: Martin Spühler, Zurich
Photo: Peter C. Horn, Stuttgart